MW01443515

Jung and the Orisha

Bridging Archetypal Psychology and African Spirituality

Jonathan Baker

Copyright © 2024 Jonathan Baker

All rights reserved. No part of this book may be reproduced, distributed, or transmitted in any form or by any means, including photocopying, recording, or other electronic or mechanical methods without written permission from the author, except for the inclusion of brief quotations in a review and certain other noncommercial uses permitted by copyright law.

ISBN-13: 9798335655187 (Paperback)
ISBN-13: 9798335655347 (Hardcover)

Library of Congress Control Number: 2024916835

Cover art by Arvin AI Art Generator
Cover design by Jonathan Baker
Chapter illustrations by Arvin AI Art Generator

Self-published in the United States of America

First printing edition 2024

Miami, Florida

*True belonging doesn't require you to change who you are;
it requires you to be who you are.*

Brené Brown

Table of Contents

Introduction to Carl Jung and His Theories 1

The Concept of Archetypes..19

The Innocent.. 25

The Orphan/Everyman 41

The Hero 55

The Caregiver...71

The Explorer 87

The Rebel 101

The Lover 115

The Creator 131

The Jester... 149

The Sage... 171

The Magician 191

The Ruler..213

The Martyr 229

Integration and Application of the Archetypes 247

Archetypal Assessment 255

Conclusion..263

Glossary 269
References 275
Index 279

Foreword

The journey through the labyrinth of human psyche and spirituality is as old as civilization itself. Among the many explorers who have charted these enigmatic terrains, Carl Jung stands as a monumental figure. His profound insights into the human mind, especially his theory of archetypes, have provided us with a compass to navigate our inner worlds. Jung's twelve archetypes—The Innocent, The Orphan/Everyman, The Hero, The Caregiver, The Explorer, The Rebel, The Lover, The Creator, The Jester, The Sage, The Magician, and The Ruler—offer a framework through which we can understand the universal patterns that shape our experiences, behaviors, and relationships.

In writing this book, my intention is to create a bridge between Jungian psychology and the rich, vibrant traditions of the Yoruba religion, specifically the Orisha. The Orisha, powerful deities in Yoruba mythology, embody a spectrum of human qualities and experiences that resonate deeply with Jung's archetypes. By examining these intersections, we gain a multifaceted understanding of how archetypal energies manifest in diverse cultural contexts, enriching our comprehension of both psychological and spiritual dimensions of life.

The Orisha are not merely mythological figures but are revered and invoked in rituals and daily life by millions of practitioners around the world. Each Orisha, with their unique attributes and stories, mirrors the complexity and richness of human nature. For instance, Oya, the fierce warrior goddess of winds and storms, embodies the resilience and transformative power of the Orphan/Everyman archetype. Her narratives of overcoming betrayal and adversity speak to the universal human experience of struggle and growth.

This book aims to delve deep into each of Jung's archetypes, correlating them with corresponding Orisha. Through detailed analyses, we explore how these archetypal energies can be understood and integrated into our lives, providing pathways for personal growth, healing, and transformation. Each chapter not only elucidates the characteristics, strengths, and shadow sides of the archetypes but also offers practical exercises and rituals inspired by the Orisha traditions. These practices are designed to help readers embody and balance these energies, promoting mental health and well-being.

In contrast to existing literature that often treats Jungian archetypes and Yoruba spirituality in isolation, this book presents a holistic and integrative approach. By weaving together psychological theories and spiritual practices, we offer readers a unique perspective that honors the wisdom of both traditions. This synthesis not only enhances our understanding of archetypes but also underscores the universality and diversity of human experiences.

The purpose of this book is not merely academic but deeply personal and transformative. It is an invitation to embark on a journey of self-discovery and empowerment, guided by the timeless wisdom of Jungian psychology and the Orisha. Whether you are a student of psychology, a practitioner of spirituality, or someone seeking deeper self-understanding, this book offers valuable insights and tools to navigate the complexities of the human soul.

As you read through these pages, may you find inspiration, clarity, and a renewed sense of connection to the archetypal energies that shape your life. May the stories and practices of the Orisha serve as a beacon, guiding you towards greater self-awareness, resilience, and harmony.

In the spirit of exploration and transformation, I invite you to delve into the world of Jungian archetypes and the Orisha, discovering the profound wisdom they offer for our contemporary lives. May this book be a companion on your journey, illuminating the path towards a more integrated and authentic self.

Welcome to the journey.

Chapter 1

Introduction to Carl Jung and His Theories

Carl Gustav Jung was born on July 26, 1875, in Kesswil, a small village in the Swiss canton of Thurgau. His early years were marked by a deep sense of isolation and a profound inner life, which he attributed to the dual influence of his father, a pastor, and his mother, who had an interest in the occult. Jung's father, Paul Achilles Jung, was a pastor in the Swiss Reformed Church, and his mother, Emilie Preiswerk Jung, came from a family with a strong tradition in spiritualism and mysticism. This blend of rational religion and mystical intuition profoundly shaped Jung's later work.

Jung pursued his medical degree at the University of Basel, where he initially showed an interest in archeology before turning to medicine. After completing his degree in 1900, he joined the Burghölzli psychiatric hospital in Zurich as an assistant to Eugen Bleuler, a pioneer in psychiatric diagnostics. It was here that Jung began his extensive work on word association tests, which laid the groundwork for his later theories on the unconscious.

In 1907, Jung met Sigmund Freud, a meeting that marked the beginning of a six-year collaboration. Freud saw in Jung a promising successor and the two exchanged numerous letters and ideas, delving deep into the unconscious mind's workings. However, fundamental differences in their views on the nature of the unconscious and the driving forces of human behavior led to their split in 1913. While Freud emphasized the sexual basis of neuroses, Jung proposed a broader understanding, incorporating a collective unconscious and a more diversified set of psychic forces.

Jung's post-Freud period was marked by intense self-reflection and exploration, often referred to as his "confrontation with the unconscious." During this time, he developed many of his key concepts, including the archetypes, the collective unconscious, and the process of individuation. He documented his inner experiences in what later became known as the *Red Book*, a compendium of visions, dreams, and symbolic paintings that illustrated his journey into the depths of the psyche.

Throughout his career, Jung published numerous influential works, including *Psychological Types* (1921), *The Archetypes and the Collective Unconscious* (1934), and *Synchronicity: An Acausal Connecting Principle* (1952). He also founded the C.G. Jung Institute in Zurich, which continues to be a center for training and research in analytical psychology. Jung's contributions to psychology extend beyond the confines of traditional psychiatry, influencing fields as diverse as anthropology, literary criticism, religious studies, and art. He passed away on June 6, 1961, leaving behind a rich legacy that continues to inspire and challenge scholars and practitioners worldwide.

OVERVIEW OF JUNGIAN PSYCHOLOGY

Jungian psychology, or analytical psychology, is a complex and multifaceted discipline that seeks to understand the totality of the human psyche. Central to Jungian thought is the concept of the unconscious, which Jung divided into the personal unconscious and the collective unconscious. The personal unconscious consists of forgotten or repressed memories and experiences unique to the individual. In contrast, the collective unconscious is a shared reservoir of experiences and knowledge inherited from our ancestors. This collective layer contains archetypes, which are universal, archaic symbols and images that manifest in dreams, myths, and cultural narratives.

One of the pivotal processes in Jungian psychology is individuation, which Jung described as the process of becoming an individual, distinct from the collective psychology. Individuation involves integrating the conscious and unconscious aspects of the self to achieve psychological wholeness. This journey towards self-realization is often depicted through the exploration of the persona, shadow, anima/animus, and the self.

The persona is the mask we wear in public, representing the roles and identities we assume to navigate social interactions. It is a necessary aspect of human life but can become problematic if we over-identify with it, leading to a disconnection from our true selves. The shadow, on the other hand, encompasses the repressed or denied parts of the self, often considered negative or undesirable. Confronting the shadow is crucial for personal growth, as it involves acknowledging and integrating these hidden aspects.

Jung also introduced the concepts of the anima and animus, which are the feminine aspects present in the male psyche and the masculine aspects present in the female psyche, respectively. These inner figures guide individuals towards a deeper understanding of their gendered selves and promote balance and harmony between the masculine and feminine energies within.

Symbols play a vital role in Jungian psychology, acting as the language of the unconscious. They appear in dreams, art, myths, and religious rituals, serving as bridges between the conscious and unconscious mind. Jung believed that symbols carry profound meanings and can provide insight into the individual's inner world and the collective human experience.

INTRODUCTION TO ARCHETYPES

Archetypes are fundamental to Jung's theory of the collective unconscious. They are innate, universal prototypes for ideas and may be used to interpret observations. Unlike Freud's concept of instincts, which are primarily biological, Jung's archetypes are more complex and multifaceted, encompassing both psychic and cultural dimensions.

One of the most recognizable archetypes is the Hero, representing the ego's quest for identity and wholeness. The Hero's journey, as articulated by Joseph Campbell, follows a pattern of departure, initiation, and return, mirroring the process of individuation. The Hero faces trials and tribulations, overcomes obstacles, and ultimately achieves a greater sense of self and purpose.

The Shadow archetype embodies the darker, repressed aspects of the psyche. It includes everything that is hidden from the conscious mind, often because it is deemed unacceptable or threatening. The process of integrating the shadow involves acknowledging these aspects and finding constructive ways to express them, leading to greater self-awareness and authenticity.

The Anima and Animus archetypes are critical in understanding gender dynamics within the psyche. The Anima represents the feminine qualities within men, such as intuition, compassion, and creativity, while the Animus represents the masculine qualities within women, such as logic, assertiveness, and strength. Balancing these inner figures is essential for psychological health and fosters a more integrated personality.

The Self archetype is the ultimate goal of individuation, representing the unified consciousness and unconsciousness of an individual. It symbolizes the totality of the psyche, encompassing all other archetypes. The Self is often depicted in mandalas, symbols of wholeness, and balance, and its realization is considered the pinnacle of personal development.

THE ORISHA

The Orisha are deities or spirits central to the Yoruba religion, which originates from the Yoruba people of West Africa. This religion has spread to various parts of the world, particularly in the Americas and the Caribbean, through the transatlantic slave trade. The Orisha are regarded as intermediaries between the human world and the divine, each embodying specific natural forces and human characteristics.

For instance, Oshun is the Orisha of love, fertility, and rivers. She is often depicted as a beautiful and sensual woman who brings fertility and prosperity. Her worship involves elaborate ceremonies and offerings, emphasizing beauty, harmony, and sweetness. Shango, another prominent Orisha, is the god of thunder, lightning, and fire. He symbolizes strength, virility, and aggression, often depicted with a double-headed axe and associated with drumming and dance. Yemaya, revered as the mother of all Orisha, represents the sea and motherhood. She is seen as a nurturing and protective figure, embodying the qualities of maternity, compassion, and care.

The Orisha are integral to the Yoruba cosmology and spiritual practice, guiding devotees through rituals, divination, and moral teachings. They are invoked for protection, healing, and guidance, playing a central role in the community's spiritual and social life.

THE ORISHA AS ARCHETYPES

In existing literature on Jungian archetypes, the focus is primarily on the twelve universal, mythic characters that Carl Jung proposed as part of his theory of the collective unconscious. These archetypes include the Innocent, the Orphan, the Hero, the Caregiver, the Explorer, the Rebel, the Lover, the Creator, the Jester, the Sage, the Magician, and the Ruler. Each archetype embodies a fundamental human motif, representing different aspects of the human experience and personality. Jungian literature delves into these archetypes through the lens of Western psychology, examining their manifestations in dreams, myths, literature, and art. The primary aim is to explore how these archetypes influence individual behavior and societal structures.

The concept of orisha as archetypes, however, introduces a unique perspective by integrating African spiritual and cultural elements into the Jungian framework. Orisha are deities in the Yoruba religion, each representing specific forces of nature and embodying distinct characteristics and virtues. For instance, Yewa is associated with purity, chastity, and the innocence of the virgin. By examining orisha through the lens of Jungian archetypes, this book aims to create a bridge between African traditional religions and Western psychology, offering a more inclusive and diverse understanding of archetypal psychology.

Similarities to Existing Literature
One major similarity is the exploration of universal themes and human experiences through archetypal figures. Both Jungian archetypes and orisha archetypes serve as symbolic representations of fundamental human traits, emotions, and life stages. For instance, the Jungian Innocent archetype represents purity, optimism, and a child-like wonder, which can be paralleled with the orisha Yewa, who embodies chastity and innocence. In both frameworks, these archetypal figures provide insights into individual behavior, cultural narratives, and the collective unconscious.

Another similarity lies in the use of myth, folklore, and cultural narratives to illustrate archetypal concepts. Jungian literature often draws from Western myths, fairy tales, and religious stories to elucidate the characteristics and roles of different archetypes. Similarly, the exploration of orisha archetypes involves delving into Yoruba myths, rituals, and oral traditions to understand the attributes and significance of each orisha. Both approaches emphasize the importance of storytelling and cultural heritage in shaping and expressing archetypal themes.

Differences from Existing Literature

A key difference between existing literature on Jungian archetypes and the concept of orisha as archetypes is the cultural context and origin of the archetypal figures. Jungian archetypes are rooted in a primarily Western, Eurocentric framework, drawing from Greek mythology, Christian theology, and European folklore. In contrast, orisha archetypes originate from the Yoruba religion and African spiritual traditions, offering a distinct cultural and historical perspective. This difference enriches the archetypal discourse by incorporating non-Western viewpoints and highlighting the diversity of human experiences and spiritual expressions.

Another difference is the integration of religious and ritualistic practices in the understanding of orisha archetypes. While Jungian literature focuses on psychological analysis and symbolic interpretation, the study of orisha archetypes involves engaging with African traditional religious practices, rituals, and ceremonies. For example, rituals dedicated to an orisha might include offerings, chants, and dances that invoke their presence and seek their blessings. These practices provide a tangible, embodied connection to the archetypal energies, which is less emphasized in the Jungian framework.

Additionally, the book aims to address contemporary issues and challenges by applying the orisha archetypes to modern contexts. For instance, understanding Yewa as an Innocent archetype can offer insights into contemporary discussions on purity, sexuality, and the sanctity of life. By drawing parallels between ancient African deities and modern psychological concepts, the book seeks to create a dialogue that resonates with today's readers and provides practical applications for personal growth and cultural understanding.

In conclusion, while the concept of orisha as archetypes shares similarities with existing literature on Jungian archetypes in terms of exploring universal themes and utilizing cultural narratives, it also presents significant differences by introducing a diverse cultural context, emphasizing religious practices, and addressing contemporary issues. This integration of African spiritual traditions with Western psychological theories enriches the discourse on archetypes and offers a more holistic and inclusive approach to understanding the complexities of the human psyche and experience.

LITERATURE REVIEW

Awo Fa'lokun Fatunmbi's *Hermeneutics - African Traditional Religions: Ifa*

Awo Fa'lokun Fatunmbi's work, *Hermeneutics - African Traditional Religions: Ifa*, provides an in-depth examination of the Ifa religious tradition and its pantheon of deities, known as the orisha. Fatunmbi's exploration is pivotal for understanding how these deities function as archetypal symbols within a psychological framework, mirroring the Jungian archetypes that serve as universal, primordial images residing in the collective unconscious.

Fatunmbi emphasizes that the orisha are not merely objects of worship but represent profound psychological and spiritual symbols that can facilitate personal transformation and healing. For instance, the orisha Ogun, associated with iron, war, and labor, is an embodiment of the Warrior archetype. Ogun's attributes of strength, resilience, and determination parallel the qualities of the Warrior archetype identified by Carl Jung. Engaging with Ogun through rituals and ceremonies allows individuals to invoke these qualities within themselves, fostering a sense of empowerment and inner strength.

Moreover, Fatunmbi's analysis highlights the therapeutic potential of the orisha. He argues that the rituals and practices associated with these deities can aid in psychological healing by allowing individuals to confront and integrate different aspects of their psyche. For example, the orisha Orunmila, who is associated with wisdom and divination, can provide guidance and clarity to individuals in times of uncertainty. This archetype aligns with the Jungian archetype of the Wise Old Man, symbolizing a source of profound knowledge and insight.

Fatunmbi's work also underscores the adaptability of the orisha within contemporary psychological practice. He illustrates how these deities can be invoked in modern therapeutic settings to address a wide range of psychological issues, from anxiety and depression to identity crises and existential dilemmas. By engaging with the orisha, individuals can access deeper layers of their unconscious, facilitating a holistic approach to healing and personal development.

In conclusion, Fatunmbi's *Hermeneutics - African Traditional Religions: Ifa* offers a rich and nuanced exploration of the orisha as archetypal symbols. His work demonstrates the profound psychological and therapeutic potential of engaging with these deities, highlighting their relevance within both traditional religious practices and modern psychological frameworks.

Moyeen Yacub's *Yoruba Mythology and Archetypal Psychology: Orisha as Transformational Symbols*

Moyeen Yacub's *Yoruba Mythology and Archetypal Psychology: Orisha as Transformational Symbols* delves into the intricate relationship between the Yoruba deities and Jungian archetypes, proposing that the orisha function as archetypal figures within the Yoruba cosmology. Yacub posits that these deities reflect the collective unconscious of the Yoruba people, embodying universal human concerns and existential dilemmas.

Yacub's analysis focuses on specific orisha and their corresponding Jungian archetypes. For instance, the orisha Eshu, known as the trickster and messenger, embodies the Trickster archetype. This archetype is central to many cultures and represents themes of duality, change, and unpredictability. Eshu's role in Yoruba mythology as a mediator and agent of change mirrors the Trickster archetype's function of disrupting the status quo and facilitating transformation. By engaging with Eshu's energy, individuals can navigate periods of upheaval and transition, ultimately emerging stronger and more resilient.

Another key figure in Yacub's work is Obatala, the god of purity and wisdom, who embodies the archetype of the Wise Old Man. Obatala's attributes of clarity, guidance, and benevolence provide a source of wisdom and stability for individuals seeking to navigate the complexities of life. Engaging with Obatala through rituals and ceremonies can help individuals connect with their inner wisdom and achieve a sense of balance and harmony.

Yacub's exploration extends to the broader cultural and psychological significance of the orisha. He argues that these deities serve as powerful symbols that inform individual and collective identity. By engaging with the orisha, individuals can access deeper layers of their psyche and connect with their cultural heritage, fostering a sense of continuity and belonging.

In conclusion, Yacub's *Yoruba Mythology and Archetypal Psychology: Orisha as Transformational Symbols* provides a comprehensive analysis of the orisha as archetypal figures. His work highlights the profound psychological and cultural significance of these deities, demonstrating their relevance within both traditional religious practices and modern psychological frameworks.

INTRODUCTION TO CARL JUNG

John Mason's *Four New World Yoruba Rituals*

John Mason's *Four New World Yoruba Rituals* offers an ethnographic perspective on the veneration of the orisha in the diaspora, particularly in the Americas. Mason provides a detailed account of the rituals and ceremonies associated with the orisha, emphasizing their role in connecting individuals to their ancestral roots and collective history.

Mason's work underscores the adaptability of the orisha in the New World context. He illustrates how these deities have been reinterpreted and integrated into various cultural and religious traditions, reflecting the dynamic nature of cultural and spiritual practices. This syncretism demonstrates the enduring relevance of the orisha as archetypal symbols that continue to resonate with individuals across different cultural landscapes.

One of the key themes in Mason's analysis is the role of the orisha in fostering community cohesion and collective identity. The rituals and ceremonies associated with these deities serve as powerful means of connecting individuals to their cultural heritage and shared history. By engaging with the archetypal figures of the orisha, individuals can bridge the gap between the personal and collective unconscious, accessing deeper layers of the psyche and fostering emotional healing and a sense of belonging.

In conclusion, Mason's *Four New World Yoruba Rituals* provides a rich ethnographic account of the veneration of the orisha in the diaspora. His work highlights the adaptability and enduring significance of these deities as archetypal symbols, demonstrating their role in fostering community cohesion and individual psychological well-being.

Adriana Facina's *Jung at the Crossroads: Reading Jung from Exu*

Adriana Facina's work *Jung at the Crossroads: Reading Jung from Exu* is an innovative exploration of the intersection between Carl Jung's analytical psychology and the Afro-Brazilian religious figure Exu. Facina delves into how the figure of Exu, a trickster deity in Afro-Brazilian and Yoruba traditions, can be interpreted through Jungian lenses, particularly regarding the archetype of the Trickster.

Facina's analysis is groundbreaking as it brings forth a cross-cultural dialogue between Jungian thought and African spiritual traditions. The text discusses how Exu's complex characteristics—simultaneously revered and feared, embodying dualities of order and chaos—resonate with Jung's concept of the Trickster archetype. Facina argues that Exu, much like the Jungian Trickster, challenges the status quo and disrupts established norms, thereby catalyzing transformation and individuation within the collective unconscious.

The book also incorporates case studies and psychoanalytic practice, demonstrating how the image and mythology of Exu can be used in therapy to address issues of identity, transformation, and personal growth. This incorporation of Exu into therapeutic practice reveals the dynamic potential of integrating culturally specific archetypes into Jungian analysis, providing a more inclusive framework for understanding the human psyche.

Facina's work contributes significantly to the ongoing discourse on the global applicability of Jungian concepts, challenging the traditionally Eurocentric focus of Jungian psychology. *Jung at the Crossroads* serves as both a critical examination of Jung's theories from an Afro-Brazilian perspective and an invitation to broaden the scope of Jungian analysis to incorporate non-Western spiritual systems. This makes Facina's work essential reading for scholars and practitioners interested in the convergence of psychoanalytic theory and African diasporic religions.

Ivor Miller's *Voice of the Leopard: African Secret Societies and Cuba*

Ivor Miller's *Voice of the Leopard: African Secret Societies and Cuba* provides a historical and cultural context for understanding the orisha as archetypes. Miller explores the transatlantic journey of the orisha and their adaptation in the New World, particularly in Afro-Caribbean religions such as Santería and Candomblé.

Miller discusses how the orisha have been reinterpreted and integrated into various cultural and religious contexts, highlighting their role in the spiritual and psychological lives of individuals in the diaspora. For example, the orisha Oshun, associated with love, beauty, and fertility, is often revered in Santería as a symbol of feminine power and sensuality. Oshun's archetypal energy resonates with individuals seeking to connect with their inner beauty and creative potential, offering a pathway to self-discovery and empowerment.

Miller's work also examines the rituals and ceremonies associated with the orisha, emphasizing their role in fostering community cohesion and collective identity. These rituals serve as powerful means of connecting individuals to their cultural heritage and shared history, providing a sense of belonging and continuity.

In conclusion, Miller's *Voice of the Leopard: African Secret Societies and Cuba* provides a comprehensive historical and cultural analysis of the orisha as archetypal figures. His work highlights the adaptability and enduring significance of these deities, demonstrating their profound impact on the spiritual and psychological lives of Afro-Caribbean communities.

Velma Love's *Divining the Self*

Velma Love's *Divining the Self: A Study in Yoruba Myth and Human Consciousness* delves into the intersections of Yoruba spirituality and personal identity, examining how engagement with orisha myths can foster self-awareness and psychological growth. Love emphasizes the transformative power of orisha narratives, suggesting that these myths serve as mirrors for the human psyche, reflecting inner conflicts and potentials.

Love focuses on the dynamic relationship between individuals and the orisha, proposing that the deities are not just external entities but also internal archetypes that reside within the collective unconscious. By exploring these inner archetypes through ritual and storytelling, individuals can gain insights into their own psychological patterns and challenges. For instance, Love discusses the orisha Oya, associated with change and transformation, as an embodiment of the transformative potential within each person. Engaging with Oya's myth can help individuals embrace change and navigate personal transitions with greater resilience and insight.

Moreover, Love's work highlights the importance of community and collective rituals in the process of self-discovery. She argues that the communal aspects of orisha worship, such as shared rituals and festivals, provide a supportive environment for individuals to explore their inner worlds and connect with their cultural heritage. These collective practices foster a sense of belonging and mutual support, which are crucial for personal and psychological well-being.

In conclusion, Love's *Divining the Self* offers a profound exploration of the orisha as archetypal figures that can guide individuals on their journeys of self-discovery and psychological transformation. Her work underscores the therapeutic potential of engaging with these deities through ritual and storytelling, highlighting their relevance within both traditional and contemporary contexts.

INTRODUCTION TO CARL JUNG

PURPOSE AND SCOPE

The primary purpose of this book is to provide a comprehensive and insightful exploration of Carl Jung's archetypes and to demonstrate the profound parallels between these archetypal figures and the orisha of the Yoruba religion. By doing so, the book aims to bridge the gap between Western psychological theories and African spiritual traditions, offering readers a unique perspective on the universal nature of archetypal symbols and their significance in both individual and collective psychological processes.

This book is designed to serve both an educational and practical function. It aims to educate readers about the fundamental concepts of Jungian psychology, including the collective unconscious, individuation, and the role of symbols and myths in personal development. By providing detailed explanations and examples, the book will help readers understand how Jung's archetypes operate within the psyche and how they influence behavior and personality.

In addition to exploring Jung's archetypes, the book delves into the rich tapestry of Yoruba mythology, focusing on the orisha as archetypal figures. Each chapter will examine specific orisha, discussing their attributes, myths, and cultural significance. This comparative analysis will illustrate how these deities function as archetypes, mirroring the themes and motifs found in Jungian psychology. For instance, Shango, the warrior-king orisha, will be compared to the Hero archetype, highlighting the universal qualities of strength, resilience, and determination. Similarly, Orunmila, the wise orisha, will be aligned with the archetype of the Sage, symbolizing guidance and profound insight.

The inclusion of the orisha as archetypes is a distinctive feature of this book, setting it apart from existing literature on Jungian psychology. While many books have explored Jung's archetypes in the context of Western myths and symbols, few have ventured into the realm of African spiritual traditions. By integrating the orisha into the discussion, this book offers a broader and more inclusive perspective on archetypal symbolism. It acknowledges the rich cultural heritage of the Yoruba religion and demonstrates the universal applicability of archetypal theory across different cultural contexts.

The scope of this book extends beyond theoretical exploration to practical application. By drawing on the works of Awo Fa'lokun Fatunmbi, Moyeen Yacub, John Mason, Adriana Facina, Ivor Miller, and Velma Love, the book provides concrete examples of how the orisha can be engaged with in therapeutic and personal development practices. For instance, Fatunmbi's analysis of Ogun as the Warrior archetype and his therapeutic potential, Yacub's exploration of Eshu as the Trickster archetype, Mason's ethnographic account of New World Yoruba rituals, Facina's integration of Exu into Jungian analysis, and Miller's historical perspective on the orisha in Afro-Caribbean contexts all contribute to a multifaceted understanding of these archetypal figures.

Furthermore, this book differentiates itself by emphasizing the therapeutic and transformative potential of engaging with archetypal symbols. It provides practical guidance on how readers can work with both Jungian archetypes and the orisha in their personal development journeys. By incorporating rituals, creative expression, and other therapeutic techniques, the book offers readers tools to access and integrate unconscious material, fostering psychological healing and spiritual growth.

In conclusion, the purpose of this book is to offer a comprehensive and inclusive exploration of Carl Jung's archetypes, demonstrating their universal nature through the comparative analysis of the Yoruba orisha. By bridging Western psychological theories and African spiritual traditions, the book aims to provide readers with a deeper understanding of archetypal symbols and their significance in both individual and collective psychological processes. Through theoretical exploration and practical application, the book seeks to educate, inspire, and empower readers on their journeys of self-discovery and personal transformation.

Chapter 2:
The Concept of Archetypes

Carl Jung's concept of archetypes is a cornerstone of his analytical psychology, a field he developed in the early 20th century. Jung's journey into the realm of archetypes began with his work at the Burghölzli psychiatric hospital in Zurich, where he collaborated with Eugen Bleuler. This period was crucial in shaping Jung's early thoughts on the unconscious mind. Through word association tests, Jung observed that patients' responses often clustered around emotionally charged complexes. These complexes, he theorized, were indicative of deeper, universal patterns within the psyche, laying the groundwork for his later work on archetypes.

Jung's break with Sigmund Freud in 1913 marked a significant turning point in his theoretical development. Freud's psychoanalytic theory focused predominantly on the personal unconscious and repressed sexuality, but Jung felt compelled to explore beyond these confines. He introduced the notion of the "collective unconscious," a concept that encompassed not only personal repressions but also a shared reservoir of experiences and symbols inherent to all humans. This idea diverged sharply from Freud's theories and allowed Jung to delve into a broader range of human experiences.

Jung's extensive study of world mythologies, religions, and cultural artifacts led him to identify recurring patterns and themes, which he termed "archetypes." In his seminal work, *The Archetypes and the Collective Unconscious* (1954), Jung argued that archetypes are primordial images and motifs that form the basic content of the collective unconscious. These archetypes, according to Jung, are not inherited ideas but predispositions to produce similar ideas or experiences. Jung identified several key archetypes, including the Hero, the Mother, the Child, and the Trickster, each representing fundamental human experiences and emotions.

Jung's exploration of alchemy further refined his understanding of archetypes. In works like *Psychology and Alchemy* (1944) and *Mysterium Coniunctionis* (1955), he saw alchemical symbols as manifestations of the individuation process, a journey toward psychological wholeness. Jung believed that the transformation depicted in alchemical texts mirrored the psyche's quest to integrate the conscious and unconscious, highlighting the archetypes' dynamic role in personal development. His insights into alchemical symbolism underscored the timeless and universal nature of archetypes, which he saw as a bridge between the individual's inner world and the collective heritage of humanity.

Collective Unconscious

The collective unconscious is one of Jung's most innovative and controversial ideas. Unlike the personal unconscious, which consists of repressed or forgotten experiences specific to an individual, the collective unconscious contains the psychic heritage of humanity. This deeper layer of the unconscious mind is composed of archetypes, universal symbols, and themes that recur across different cultures and epochs. Jung described the collective unconscious as a repository of latent memories from our ancestral past, not directly accessible but influential in our thoughts, behaviors, and perceptions.

The concept of the collective unconscious emerged from Jung's studies of ancient myths, religions, and cultural practices. He observed that certain symbols and motifs appeared consistently across different civilizations, despite geographical and temporal separations. For example, the archetype of the Mother appears universally, symbolizing nurturing, protection, and fertility. This archetype manifests in various cultural forms, such as the Virgin Mary in Christianity, Isis in Egyptian mythology, and Demeter in Greek mythology, each embodying the maternal essence.

THE CONCEPT OF ARCHETYPES

The Hero archetype is another powerful example, embodying the individual's quest for identity and self-realization. The Hero's journey, popularized by Joseph Campbell in *The Hero with a Thousand Faces* (1949), illustrates a universal pattern of departure, initiation, and return. This narrative structure is found in myths, religious texts, and contemporary stories, reflecting the collective unconscious's influence on human storytelling. Jung's analysis of these myths revealed that the Hero's journey represents an individual's struggle to overcome inner and outer challenges, leading to personal growth and transformation.

Dreams are a primary means through which the collective unconscious communicates with the conscious mind. Jungian therapy often involves dream analysis to uncover the archetypal themes and symbols that reveal the patient's inner conflicts and potential paths for growth. Jung believed that engaging with these archetypal images could facilitate the individuation process, helping individuals integrate disparate parts of their psyche. For example, recurring dreams of a protective figure might indicate the presence of the Wise Old Man or the Great Mother archetype, guiding the dreamer towards wisdom and nurturing.

Symbols and Myths
Symbols and myths play a crucial role in Jungian psychology, acting as the language of the unconscious. Jung saw symbols as dynamic, multifaceted images that convey meanings beyond the literal and the rational. They are the psyche's way of expressing complex, often contradictory aspects of the self and the world. Symbols are not static; their meanings evolve as individuals and cultures change, reflecting the dynamic interplay between the conscious and unconscious mind.

Myths, in Jung's view, are collective dreams of a culture. They encapsulate the shared experiences and values of a community, providing a narrative framework for understanding the human condition. Myths are rich in archetypal imagery, offering insights into the collective unconscious's workings. For example, the Greek myth of Persephone's descent into the underworld and her eventual return to the surface symbolizes the cyclical nature of life, death, and rebirth, reflecting the archetype of the Journey and Transformation. This myth, like many others, provides a profound commentary on the human experience of loss, renewal, and the eternal cycle of change.

Dreams, like myths, are laden with symbolic content. Jungian analysts interpret dreams by identifying the archetypal themes and symbols that emerge from the unconscious. For instance, dreaming of a house might symbolize the self, with different rooms representing various aspects of the dreamer's personality. A dream of flying could indicate a desire for freedom or a transcendence of earthly concerns, drawing on the archetype of the Spirit or the transcendent Self. Jung believed that by understanding these symbols, individuals could gain deeper insights into their unconscious motivations and conflicts.

Art and religious rituals are also replete with archetypal symbols. Jung's analysis of mandalas, circular designs often used in Hindu and Buddhist practices, revealed their significance as symbols of the Self and wholeness. He found similar motifs in medieval Christian alchemical texts and modern patients' drawings, underscoring the universality of these images. Jung's work with patients often involved encouraging them to create their own mandalas as a way to explore and integrate their unconscious material. This practice highlighted the therapeutic potential of engaging with archetypal symbols.

Importance of Archetypes in Personal Development
Archetypes significantly influence behavior and personality, guiding individuals through various stages of life and psychological growth. Understanding and engaging with these archetypal patterns can lead to greater self-awareness and personal development. Jung believed that

recognizing and integrating archetypal energies was essential for achieving psychological balance and wholeness.

One of the primary ways archetypes shape behavior is through the individuation process, which Jung described as the integration of the conscious and unconscious parts of the psyche. This journey involves encountering and reconciling various archetypes, such as the Shadow, the Anima/Animus, and the Self. Confronting the Shadow, for example, requires acknowledging and integrating the repressed, often darker aspects of the self. This process can be challenging but ultimately leads to a more authentic and balanced personality. The Shadow represents the parts of ourselves that we deny or ignore, and by facing it, we can transform these aspects into sources of strength and creativity.

The Anima and Animus archetypes play a crucial role in personal relationships and inner balance. For men, the Anima represents the inner feminine qualities, such as empathy and intuition, while for women, the Animus embodies the inner masculine traits, such as assertiveness and rationality. Recognizing and integrating these opposite-gendered aspects can enhance psychological wholeness and improve interpersonal dynamics. Jung believed that failing to integrate these aspects could lead to projections, where individuals see their Anima or Animus qualities in others, often resulting in idealization or conflict.

The Self archetype, which symbolizes the totality of the psyche, represents the ultimate goal of individuation. Realizing the Self involves harmonizing all parts of the personality, leading to a sense of inner peace and completeness. Jung believed that symbols of the Self, such as mandalas, could facilitate this process by providing a visual representation of wholeness. The Self is not just the sum of the conscious and unconscious parts of the psyche; it also includes the potential for growth and transformation, guiding individuals towards their highest potential.

Archetypes also influence career choices, creative expression, and spiritual practices. The Hero archetype, for instance, might inspire individuals to pursue careers that involve challenge and adventure, while the Caregiver archetype might lead to professions in healthcare or social services. Artists often draw on archetypal images to convey universal themes and emotions, while spiritual seekers might find meaning in rituals and symbols that resonate with their inner archetypes. Understanding these influences can help individuals make more informed and fulfilling life choices, aligning their actions with their deepest values and aspirations.

By exploring and understanding the archetypal dimensions of their psyche, individuals can gain valuable insights into their motivations, fears, and aspirations. This self-knowledge can empower them to make more informed and fulfilling life choices, fostering personal growth and well-being. Jung's emphasis on the importance of archetypes in personal development underscores the transformative potential of engaging with the deeper layers of the unconscious mind.

As we conclude our exploration of the foundational concepts of archetypes within Jungian psychology, we recognize the profound impact these universal symbols have on both individual psyches and collective cultural narratives. With this understanding as our backdrop, the following chapters of this book are dedicated to an in-depth examination of each of the twelve archetypes. We will explore their unique characteristics, strengths, weaknesses, and the roles they play in personal development and societal structures. Alongside this analysis, we will also delve into the fascinating realm of Yoruba spirituality, aligning each archetype with its corresponding orisha. This comparative approach not only enriches our understanding of archetypes but also bridges diverse cultural perspectives, highlighting the universal themes that transcend geographical and spiritual boundaries. As we transition into these detailed discussions, each chapter will offer insights into how these archetypal energies manifest in our lives and guide us on our paths to self-realization and transformation.

Chapter 3

The Innocent

The Innocent archetype, one of Carl Jung's twelve primary archetypes, is characterized by its profound optimism, simplicity, and trust. This archetype embodies a childlike purity and a sense of wonder, seeing the world through a lens of unblemished hope and positivity. The Innocent believes in the inherent goodness of people and the world, striving for a life that is free from the complexities and corruptions of modern existence. This archetype values simplicity and seeks to find joy in the small, everyday aspects of life. The Innocent's outlook is often idealistic, aiming to achieve a utopian vision of life where harmony and happiness reign supreme.

The Innocent's trust in others is absolute, often leading them to be perceived as naive or overly simplistic. However, this unwavering faith in the good is what defines the essence of the Innocent archetype. They tend to approach life with a sense of curiosity and openness, eager to explore and experience without the burdens of doubt and cynicism. This archetype's primary motivation is to be happy and to spread happiness, making them an endearing and inspiring presence in any narrative or real-life scenario.

Strengths and Weaknesses

The strengths of the Innocent archetype lie in its boundless positivity and ability to inspire others. The Innocent's optimism can be infectious, encouraging those around them to adopt a more hopeful and trusting perspective. This archetype is often a source of comfort and reassurance, reminding others of the simple joys and fundamental goodness of life. The Innocent's trust and openness can also lead to deep and meaningful connections with others, as their lack of guile or suspicion fosters an environment of genuine interaction and mutual support.

However, the Innocent's strengths are also the source of its greatest weaknesses. The archetype's unwavering trust can sometimes lead to gullibility, making the Innocent vulnerable to manipulation and deceit. Their idealistic nature can result in a lack of preparedness for the harsher realities of life, leaving them ill-equipped to deal with conflict, disappointment, or betrayal. The Innocent's simplicity, while endearing, can also be perceived as a lack of depth or sophistication, potentially leading to underestimation or dismissal by others.

Cultural Examples

The Innocent archetype is prevalent in literature, film, and mythology, serving as a symbol of hope and purity across various narratives. In literature, characters such as Pip in Charles Dickens' *Great Expectations* and Anne Shirley in L.M. Montgomery's *Anne of Green Gables* exemplify the Innocent archetype. Pip's initial idealism and trust in the world around him and Anne's unwavering optimism and imagination highlight the core traits of this archetype.

In film, characters like Dorothy in *The Wizard of Oz* and Amélie in *Amélie* embody the Innocent archetype. Dorothy's journey through Oz is driven by her simple desire to return home and her belief in the goodness of the friends she meets along the way. Amélie's whimsical approach to life and her efforts to bring joy to those around her showcase the Innocent's inherent positivity and trust.

Mythological figures such as Persephone from Greek mythology also reflect the Innocent archetype. Persephone's initial innocence and purity, coupled with her eventual abduction by Hades, underscore the archetype's vulnerability and the potential for its exploitation. Despite her ordeal, Persephone retains her core qualities of hope and renewal, embodying the resilience of the Innocent archetype.

Historical or Contemporary Figures
Anne Frank (1929–1945)
Anne Frank, the Jewish teenager who wrote *The Diary of a Young Girl* while hiding from the Nazis during World War II, epitomizes the Innocent archetype. Despite the horrors surrounding her, Anne maintained an optimistic outlook on life and humanity. Her writings reveal a hopeful spirit, even in the face of unimaginable adversity. Anne's innocence, coupled with her profound belief in the goodness of people, remains an inspiring testament to the power of hope and resilience in dark times.

Mahatma Gandhi (1869–1948)
Mahatma Gandhi, the leader of the Indian independence movement against British rule, also embodies the Innocent archetype. Gandhi's approach to political activism was rooted in nonviolence (ahimsa) and a belief in the inherent goodness of humanity. His unwavering commitment to truth and nonviolent resistance, even when faced with oppression and violence, highlights the Innocent's potential for powerful, transformative influence.

In Psychology
Furthermore, the Innocent archetype appears in contemporary psychology, where it is associated with the childlike aspects of the human psyche, emphasizing the importance of maintaining a sense of wonder and hope. This archetype is often invoked in therapeutic settings to help individuals

reconnect with their inner child, fostering resilience and emotional healing by reminding them of the inherent goodness and simplicity that can still be found within. The resurgence of mindfulness practices, which encourage living in the present moment with an open and non-judgmental mind, also speaks to the influence of the Innocent archetype in modern life.

Shadow Side

The shadow side of the Innocent archetype manifests in the form of denial, avoidance, and naivety. When confronted with the darker aspects of reality, the Innocent may retreat into denial, refusing to acknowledge or address unpleasant truths. This avoidance can lead to a lack of growth and self-awareness, as the Innocent fails to confront and integrate the more challenging aspects of their psyche and environment.

Naivety, while often seen as a charming trait, can also result in significant personal and interpersonal difficulties. The Innocent's tendency to trust unconditionally can make them susceptible to manipulation and betrayal, leading to disillusionment and a potential loss of faith in others. This vulnerability underscores the importance of balancing the Innocent's optimism with a healthy dose of realism and discernment.

Furthermore, the Innocent's simplicity can sometimes be perceived as a lack of depth or complexity, potentially leading to misunderstandings or underestimation by others. This perception can result in the Innocent being marginalized or overlooked in situations that require more nuanced or sophisticated approaches.

Path to Individuation

Individuation, according to Jungian psychology, is the process of integrating various aspects of the psyche to achieve a balanced and whole self. For the Innocent archetype, this path involves learning to balance their inherent optimism and trust with a realistic understanding of the world. The Innocent must develop discernment, learning to recognize and navigate the complexities and potential dangers of their environment without losing their core sense of hope and positivity.

Engaging with the Innocent archetype in a conscious and intentional way can facilitate this process. Practices such as mindfulness, reflection, and boundary-setting can help the Innocent develop greater self-awareness and resilience. By acknowledging and integrating their shadow side, the Innocent can achieve a more balanced and grounded perspective, allowing them to navigate life's challenges with both optimism and wisdom.

The journey of individuation for the Innocent also involves embracing the orisha who best embodies this archetype.

YEWA AS THE INNOCENT

Yewa, also known as Yewá, is one of the most venerated orisha in the Yoruba pantheon. She embodies the Innocent archetype through her association with purity, chastity, and her guardianship of the dead. Her narrative highlights the themes of innocence, transformation, and the quest for moral integrity, making her a powerful symbol for those seeking to understand and connect with the Innocent archetype.

Characteristics and Traits
Yewa is revered as the orisha of the Yewa River and the goddess of chastity and purity. Her domain over the cemetery and the realm of the dead signifies her role as a protector of souls and a guide in the transition between life and death. Yewa's presence is marked by her grace, humility, and an unwavering commitment to maintaining her purity, traits that are central to the Innocent archetype. She embodies the qualities of optimism, trust, and simplicity, often depicted as a gentle and nurturing figure who cares deeply for those under her protection.

Yewa's innocence is not naive or simplistic; rather, it represents a profound understanding of the cyclical nature of life and death. Her association with the cemetery symbolizes a deep connection to the spiritual realm and an awareness of life's impermanence, which guides her actions and decisions. Through her narrative, Yewa teaches that innocence can be a source of strength and resilience, allowing individuals to navigate life's challenges with grace and dignity.

Strengths and Weaknesses
Yewa's strengths lie in her purity and her ability to maintain a sense of hope and optimism in the face of adversity. Her innocence allows her to see the world through a lens of possibility and potential, inspiring those around her to embrace their own inner light. This quality can be empowering, providing a sense of clarity and purpose even in the darkest times. Yewa's commitment to purity and her role as a guardian also highlight her strength in maintaining boundaries and upholding values, serving as a reminder of the importance of integrity and ethical conduct.

However, Yewa's innocence can also be a source of vulnerability. Her desire to see the best in others may lead to disillusionment or disappointment when faced with deception or betrayal. This potential for naivety can make her susceptible to manipulation, particularly when her ideals are challenged. The Innocent archetype must learn to balance their optimism with discernment, recognizing that not all intentions are pure and that wisdom comes from experience as much as from virtue.

Shadow Side
The shadow side of Yewa, as with any Innocent archetype, emerges when her purity becomes rigid and unyielding, leading to self-righteousness or judgmental attitudes. In her quest to maintain innocence, Yewa may inadvertently isolate herself, avoiding situations or relationships that challenge her ideals. This avoidance can manifest as fear of change or an

unwillingness to confront difficult truths, limiting her ability to grow and adapt.

Additionally, Yewa's emphasis on chastity and purity may lead to self-denial or repression, where her natural desires are suppressed in favor of maintaining an image of perfection. This can create internal conflict and result in feelings of inadequacy or shame when her human imperfections are exposed. It is essential for Yewa, and those who embody her archetype, to embrace their vulnerabilities and imperfections, recognizing that true innocence is not the absence of flaws but the acceptance and integration of them.

Path to Individuation
The path to individuation for Yewa involves embracing the balance between innocence and experience, allowing her to integrate her ideals with the realities of life. This journey requires developing discernment and learning to trust her intuition, helping her navigate the complexities of human relationships and societal expectations. By cultivating self-awareness and accepting her vulnerabilities, Yewa can maintain her purity while growing into a more nuanced and resilient version of herself.

For Yewa, individuation is about finding harmony between her role as a guardian of the dead and her own personal growth. It involves honoring her connection to the spiritual realm while engaging with the world around her, allowing her experiences to inform and deepen her understanding of life's cycles. By embracing her path and learning to balance her ideals with reality, Yewa can embody the true essence of the Innocent archetype: a figure of hope, transformation, and enduring grace.

YEWA STORIES

Yewa's Chastity

Yewa, also known as Yewá, is revered as an orisha of fertility, purity, and the Yewa River (Odò Yewa), often depicted as a paragon of chastity and virtue in Yoruba mythology. Her commitment to maintaining her virginity was not only a personal vow but also a sacred duty that symbolized her purity and dedication to her divine role. According to myth, Yewa's chastity was integral to her power and status among the orisha, setting her apart as a beacon of moral and spiritual integrity.

Yewa's story of chastity is deeply interwoven with the themes of purity and sacrifice. As the goddess of fertility and the earth, her virginity was believed to be a source of her strength, enabling her to bestow life and nurture the natural world without the influence of mortal desires or distractions. Her purity was a testament to her unwavering commitment to her divine responsibilities, and she was venerated for her ability to maintain this sacred state amidst the complexities of life.

The Encounter with Shango

The narrative takes a dramatic turn with the arrival of Shango, the orisha of thunder, lightning, and fire. Shango is known for his charismatic and passionate nature, often depicted as a figure of immense power and irresistible allure. His presence in Yewa's life marked a significant and tumultuous chapter in her mythology, highlighting the tensions between duty and desire, purity and passion.

The encounter between Yewa and Shango is described as a moment of intense attraction and vulnerability. Despite her vow of chastity, Yewa found herself irresistibly drawn to Shango's magnetic presence. The allure of Shango, coupled with his assertive and persuasive nature, eventually led Yewa to break her vow. In a moment of profound emotional and spiritual conflict, Yewa succumbed to Shango's advances, and they consummated their relationship, resulting in the loss of her virginity.

Repercussions of Yewa's Decision

The repercussions of Yewa's decision were immediate and severe. In the aftermath of her union with Shango, Yewa faced significant ostracism and condemnation from the other orisha. Her loss of virginity was seen as a profound transgression, not only of her personal vow but also of the sacred duties and responsibilities she upheld. The purity that had once defined her divine essence was now called into question, leading to a dramatic shift in her status and perception among her peers.

Yewa's fall from grace serves as a poignant reminder of the rigid expectations and harsh judgments that often accompany notions of purity and virtue. Despite her profound contributions to the natural world and her unwavering dedication to her divine role, Yewa was subjected to a harsh and unforgiving scrutiny that overshadowed her previous accomplishments and sacrifices. Some accounts state that she was banished to live the rest of her days in the cemetery to better uphold her vows of celibacy, as this was the one place Shango was afraid to visit.

The mythology surrounding Yewa's relationship with Shango and its aftermath highlights the complex interplay between divine duties and personal desires. It underscores the challenges faced by those who seek to maintain purity and integrity in the face of overwhelming temptation and the severe consequences that can follow from a single transgression.

Reflection on Yewa's Story

Yewa's story is a powerful exploration of the themes of purity, sacrifice, and the consequences of moral and spiritual transgressions. It serves as a rich source of archetypal imagery, illustrating the tensions and conflicts that arise from the pursuit of an idealized state of virtue and the harsh realities that can accompany deviations from this path.

In the context of the Innocent archetype, Yewa's narrative provides a compelling illustration of the vulnerability and resilience inherent in this archetype. Her initial purity and dedication to her sacred duties exemplify the Innocent's idealism and commitment to a higher moral standard. However, her eventual succumbing to desire and the subsequent repercussions reflect the Innocent's potential for naivety and the harsh consequences that can follow from a loss of innocence.

By examining Yewa's story through the lens of the Innocent archetype, we gain a deeper understanding of the complexities and challenges associated with maintaining purity and integrity in a world fraught with temptation and moral ambiguity. Yewa's journey underscores the importance of resilience and self-forgiveness in the face of transgressions, highlighting the need to balance idealism with a realistic understanding of human nature and the inevitability of mistakes.

In the context of modern psychological practice, engaging with Yewa can provide valuable insights and healing. Her archetypal energy can help individuals navigate the complexities of life with a sense of hope and trust. By invoking her qualities through rituals, meditation, or creative expression, individuals can access deeper layers of their psyche and foster a sense of wholeness and balance.

EXERCISES & RITUALS

Morning Gratitude Ritual

Supplies Needed:
- A journal or notebook
- A pen
- A quiet, comfortable space

Steps:
1. Begin by finding a quiet and comfortable space where you can sit undisturbed for a few minutes.
2. Take a few deep breaths, inhaling through your nose and exhaling through your mouth, to center yourself and clear your mind.
3. Open your journal or notebook and write down three things you are grateful for. These can be simple things like the warmth of the sun, a good meal, or a kind gesture from a friend.
4. Reflect on each item you've written, allowing yourself to feel the gratitude and joy that each brings.
5. Close your journal, take a few more deep breaths, and set an intention to carry this feeling of gratitude with you throughout the day.

Explanation:
Practicing gratitude helps align with the Innocent Archetype by fostering a sense of optimism and appreciation for the simple joys in life. It helps shift focus from negativity to positivity, promoting mental well-being and a sense of fulfillment.

Purity Cleansing Ritual

Supplies Needed:
- A small bowl of water
- A few drops of lavender or rose essential oil
- A white cloth or towel

Steps:
1. Fill a small bowl with water and add a few drops of lavender or rose essential oil.
2. Sit quietly in a comfortable space and take a few deep breaths to center yourself.

3. Dip the white cloth into the scented water and gently wipe your face, hands, and feet.
4. As you cleanse, imagine washing away any negative energy or impurities, leaving you feeling refreshed and purified.
5. Take a few more deep breaths, and visualize yourself surrounded by a white, purifying light.

Explanation:
This cleansing ritual aligns with Yewa's aspect of purity and the Innocent Archetype's focus on simplicity and renewal. It can help release negative energy, promote a sense of freshness and clarity, and enhance overall well-being.

Inner Child Visualization

Supplies Needed:
- A quiet, comfortable space
- A journal or notebook
- A pen

Steps:
1. Find a quiet and comfortable space where you won't be disturbed.
2. Close your eyes and take several deep breaths to relax and center yourself.
3. Visualize yourself as a child, perhaps at a time when you felt happy and carefree.
4. Imagine this child version of yourself in a safe, nurturing environment. Observe what they are doing, how they are feeling, and what brings them joy.
5. Spend a few minutes connecting with your inner child, offering them love, compassion, and reassurance.

6. After the visualization, open your journal and write about your experience. Reflect on any insights or emotions that arose during the exercise.

Explanation:
Connecting with your inner child helps align with the Innocent Archetype by fostering a sense of purity, joy, and openness. This exercise can promote emotional healing, self-compassion, and a deeper understanding of your core needs and desires.

Solitude and Reflection in Nature

Supplies Needed:
- Comfortable clothing
- A journal or notebook
- A pen
- A natural setting such as a park, forest, or garden

Steps:
1. Dress in comfortable clothing and find a natural setting where you can be alone and undisturbed.
2. Bring your journal or notebook and a pen with you.
3. Spend some time walking or sitting in nature, observing the beauty and tranquility around you.
4. Choose a quiet spot where you feel comfortable and at peace.
5. Open your journal and write about your thoughts, feelings, and reflections on the themes of innocence, purity, and simplicity.
6. Allow yourself to be fully present in the moment, embracing the solitude and the connection with the natural world.
7. Spend at least 30 minutes to an hour in this reflective practice, letting nature inspire your thoughts and emotions.

Explanation:
Spending time alone in nature promotes a sense of innocence and purity by allowing you to connect with the simplicity and beauty of the natural world. It encourages introspection, mindfulness, and emotional healing, fostering a deeper sense of inner peace and well-being.

REFLECTIONS

Yewa's poignant story within the Yoruba pantheon deeply embodies the Innocent archetype, marked by themes of purity, vulnerability, and the transformational challenges that test these qualities. As the orisha of purity and the protector of the dead, Yewa's narrative offers a compelling exploration of the Innocent's journey through life's inevitable complexities and moral dilemmas.

Her tale, particularly the tragic elements surrounding the loss of her virginity and the subsequent retreat to the cemetery, highlights the fragility and the strength inherent in the Innocent archetype. Yewa's experiences reflect the profound impact of innocence confronted with the harsh realities of the world, and her response to these challenges is a testament to the resilience that can emerge from vulnerability.

Yewa's eventual role as a guardian of the cemetery symbolizes a transformative acceptance and adaptation to her circumstances, illustrating how even the most Innocent among us can find strength in adversity and redefine their role in meaningful ways. Her story encourages those who resonate with the Innocent archetype to embrace their purity not as a weakness but as a source of strength and clarity, guiding them through life's trials with integrity and grace.

Her narrative also serves as a reminder of the protective measures that the Innocent must take to safeguard their virtues while navigating a world that may not always honor them. It teaches the importance of setting boundaries

THE INNOCENT

and finding safe spaces where one's innocence can be a source of empowerment rather than a point of vulnerability.

Let Yewa's journey inspire those aligned with the Innocent archetype to approach the world with open eyes and a steadfast heart, recognizing that purity of spirit can coexist with the wisdom gained through experience. Her evolution from innocence to protective guardian shows that even the most tender qualities can develop into formidable strengths, enabling individuals to protect themselves and others. Through her, we learn that innocence, when nurtured and wisely managed, can lead to profound growth and unexpected leadership, preserving one's core integrity along the way.

Chapter 4

The Orphan/Everyman

The Orphan/Everyman archetype represents the quintessential human experience of belonging, realism, empathy, and connection. This archetype speaks to the universal desire for acceptance and the deep-rooted need to find one's place in the world. Understanding this archetype involves exploring its characteristics, strengths, weaknesses, cultural manifestations, shadow side, and the path to individuation. Additionally, this chapter will delve into the orisha Oya, demonstrating how she embodies the Orphan/Everyman archetype through her narratives and attributes.

Characteristics and Traits

The Orphan/Everyman archetype is grounded in realism, emphasizing the ordinary, the humble, and the relatable aspects of human life. Individuals who resonate with this archetype value authenticity and honesty, often finding solace in shared experiences and common struggles. They exhibit a profound sense of empathy, understanding others' pain and joy through their own experiences. Connection is paramount to the Orphan/Everyman, as they seek to form meaningful relationships that affirm their sense of belonging and community.

In literature and psychology, the Orphan/Everyman is often depicted as a character who navigates life's challenges with a pragmatic outlook. They are realistic, sometimes to a fault, acknowledging the harsh truths of existence without losing hope in the potential for human kindness and solidarity. This archetype embodies the notion that, despite life's adversities, we are all in this together.

Strengths and Weaknesses
The strengths of the Orphan/Everyman archetype lie in their groundedness and their ability to relate to others. Their realistic perspective enables them to handle life's ups and downs with a steady hand. They are often seen as the glue that holds groups together, providing support and understanding when needed. Their empathy allows them to connect deeply with others, fostering a sense of trust and mutual respect.

However, this archetype also has its weaknesses. The Orphan/Everyman can sometimes feel overwhelmed by their own sense of victimization, particularly when faced with situations that highlight their vulnerabilities or marginalization. This feeling of being perpetually downtrodden can lead to a sense of hopelessness and resignation. When the shadow side of this archetype takes over, the individual may become cynical, excessively self-pitying, or overly reliant on others for validation and support.

Cultural Examples
The Orphan/Everyman archetype is pervasive in cultural narratives, from classic literature to modern films. In Charles Dickens' *Oliver Twist*, the character of Oliver embodies the Orphan archetype, navigating a harsh world with resilience and hope for a better life. In modern cinema, the Everyman can be seen in characters like Frodo Baggins from *The Lord of the Rings*, whose ordinary beginnings contrast with the extraordinary journey he undertakes, emphasizing the heroism found in the everyday person.

Mythology also offers rich examples of this archetype. In Greek mythology, figures like Odysseus exemplify the Everyman through their relatable struggles and triumphs. Odysseus' journey is marked by a series of realistic challenges and encounters that highlight human vulnerability and resilience. These cultural representations underscore the timeless appeal and relatability of the Orphan/Everyman archetype.

Historical or Contemporary Figures
Charles Dickens (1812–1870)
Charles Dickens, the renowned English author, often wrote about characters who embody the Orphan/Everyman archetype. In works like *Oliver Twist* and *David Copperfield*, Dickens explored themes of poverty, alienation, and resilience. His characters, often orphans or marginalized individuals, reflect the Everyman's struggle for survival, belonging, and dignity in a harsh and unjust world.

Harriet Tubman (c. 1822–1913)
Harriet Tubman, an American abolitionist and political activist, is a quintessential example of the Orphan/Everyman archetype. Born into slavery, Tubman escaped and then led numerous missions to rescue enslaved people through the Underground Railroad. Her life and work exemplify the Everyman's journey from hardship to empowerment, showing how ordinary individuals can make extraordinary impacts.

In Psychology
In modern psychology, the Orphan/Everyman archetype is often explored through the lens of attachment theory and the importance of social connections. Therapists may work with clients to address feelings of abandonment or isolation, helping them to build stronger interpersonal relationships and a sense of belonging. Additionally, the archetype's emphasis on empathy and solidarity is reflected in the increasing focus on social justice and advocacy, where individuals and groups strive to create a more inclusive and equitable society. The Orphan/Everyman archetype

encourages us to see ourselves in others and to work together to overcome shared challenges.

Shadow Side
The shadow side of the Orphan/Everyman archetype emerges when the individual's sense of realism turns into cynicism and defeatism. When overwhelmed by the weight of their own struggles or the perceived indifference of the world, they may withdraw into a state of self-pity and helplessness. This negative manifestation can lead to a victim mentality, where the individual feels powerless to change their circumstances and becomes overly dependent on others for emotional support.

In extreme cases, the Orphan/Everyman may sabotage their own potential by refusing to take risks or pursue opportunities for fear of failure or rejection. Their empathy, while a strength, can also become a burden when they internalize the pain and suffering of others to an unhealthy degree, leading to emotional burnout and compassion fatigue. Recognizing and addressing these shadow aspects is crucial for achieving balance and personal growth.

Path to Individuation
The path to individuation for the Orphan/Everyman archetype involves embracing both their strengths and weaknesses to achieve a harmonious and authentic self. This journey requires the individual to acknowledge their vulnerabilities without succumbing to a victim mentality. Building resilience and self-compassion is key, allowing them to navigate life's challenges with a balanced perspective.

Practical steps towards individuation include fostering self-awareness through mindfulness and reflection. Engaging in activities that promote self-care and emotional well-being, such as journaling, therapy, and supportive social interactions, can help the Orphan/Everyman maintain a healthy outlook. Additionally, setting realistic goals and celebrating small achievements can boost their sense of agency and confidence.

Connecting with the orisha Oya can provide further guidance and inspiration. Oya, known as the orisha of winds, storms, and transformation, embodies the strength and resilience of the Orphan/Everyman archetype. Despite her tumultuous nature, Oya is a figure of profound empathy and connection, guiding those who seek her wisdom through life's inevitable changes.

OYA AS THE ORPHAN/EVERYMAN

Oya, the fierce Orisha of winds and storms, epitomizes the Orphan/Everyman archetype through her multifaceted nature and experiences of vulnerability, resilience, and transformation. Known for her strength and tenacity, Oya confronts numerous trials and tribulations, often surmounting them with determination and grace. Her guardianship over cemeteries and the dead underscores her deep connection to life's transitional phases and the collective human experience.

Characteristics and Traits
Oya is revered as a fierce and protective deity who governs the winds and storms. Her presence is both formidable and nurturing, embodying the duality of strength and empathy. As the orisha of transformation, Oya guides individuals through significant life changes, helping them navigate the turbulent waters of existence with resilience and courage. Her ability to bring about change and renewal aligns with the Orphan/Everyman's capacity for adaptation and growth.

Strengths and Weaknesses
Oya's strengths lie in her transformative power and her deep empathy for human struggles. She is a protector of those who are marginalized and vulnerable, offering her guidance and support to those in need. Oya's

connection to the cemetery and the ancestors further underscores her role as a bridge between the living and the spiritual realms, emphasizing the Orphan/Everyman's desire for connection and belonging.

However, Oya's association with storms and upheaval also highlights her potential weaknesses. Her transformative energy can be overwhelming, leading to periods of intense emotional turbulence for those she guides. This aspect of Oya's nature mirrors the Orphan/Everyman's tendency to feel victimized or overwhelmed by life's challenges. Balancing her fierce strength with compassion and stability is essential for those who seek her wisdom.

Shadow Side
The shadow side of Oya manifests in her association with destructive storms and upheaval. While her transformative energy is essential for growth, it can also lead to periods of chaos and instability. Individuals who align with Oya may struggle with intense emotions and the fear of being overwhelmed by life's challenges. This shadow aspect reflects the Orphan/Everyman's potential for feeling victimized or powerless in the face of adversity.

Recognizing and integrating Oya's shadow side involves embracing the transformative power of change while maintaining a sense of grounding and stability. It requires acknowledging the storms within and finding ways to harness their energy for positive growth and renewal.

Path to Individuation
Working with Oya as a guide on the path to individuation involves embracing her transformative energy and her deep empathy. Rituals and exercises that honor Oya's connection to the winds, storms, and ancestors can help individuals align with her wisdom and strength. Practices such as spending time in nature, especially during windy or stormy weather, can foster a sense of connection to Oya's energy and the natural world.

Additionally, rituals that involve honoring the ancestors and visiting cemeteries with respect and reverence can deepen the connection to Oya and the Orphan/Everyman archetype. Offering fresh flowers, lighting candles, and reflecting on the stories and legacies of those who have passed can provide a sense of continuity and belonging.

OYA STORIES

In Yoruba mythology, Oya is celebrated for her significant roles in both the natural and spiritual worlds, often depicted as a formidable warrior wielding a machete and commanding the winds. Her myths emphasize her transformative power and ability to guide souls through the transition from life to death, underscoring her connection to the cemetery and ancestors as a guardian of the departed and a mediator between realms. A notable myth involving Oya is her marriage to Shango, the orisha of thunder and lightning, representing the dynamic interplay of powerful forces in nature and human experience. Oya's stories are rich with themes of resilience, transformation, and the pursuit of justice, resonating deeply with the Orphan/Everyman archetype's quest for meaning and connection.

Oya's journey is marked by significant trials, including her tumultuous relationship with Shango, the Orisha of thunder. Their relationship is characterized by passion and conflict, reflecting the Everyman's struggle with life's challenges. In one story, Oya disguises herself as a buffalo to escape a hunter's advances, only to be coerced into marriage when he discovers her secret. This tale highlights her vulnerability and the difficulties she faces in maintaining her autonomy and strength.

Another critical aspect of Oya's narrative involves her conflict with Osanyin, the Orisha of herbal medicine. Osanyin, possessing vast knowledge of the healing properties of plants, was known for his reclusive and secretive nature. According to one story, Oya, desiring to learn the secrets of healing to aid her community, approached Osanyin. However, Osanyin refused to share his knowledge, viewing it as his exclusive domain. In response, Oya, determined and resourceful, summoned a powerful storm that uprooted many of Osanyin's plants and scattered them across the land. This act symbolized the democratization of knowledge, making the healing properties of plants accessible to all. Oya's defiance and innovative approach in the face of rejection highlight her alignment with the Everyman archetype's groundedness and empathy.

Oya's relationship with Osanyin also underscores the themes of betrayal and resilience. After scattering the plants, Osanyin sought to punish Oya, but she remained steadfast, demonstrating her resilience and commitment to her community. This conflict mirrors the Everyman's experiences of betrayal and the struggle for empowerment in the face of adversity. Oya's ability to transform adversity into empowerment resonates deeply with the Everyman archetype, as she navigates life's complexities with a realistic perspective, finding strength in her connections to both the spiritual and physical realms.

These stories of Oya's trials, from her passionate and volatile relationship with Shango to her defiant conflict with Osanyin, illustrate her embodiment of the Orphan/Everyman archetype. Her journey encourages individuals to embrace their vulnerabilities and seek strength in community and self-awareness. By aligning with Oya and the Orphan/Everyman archetype, individuals can find inspiration in her resilience and transformative power. Engaging with her stories and rituals can help individuals cultivate empathy, strength, and a deeper understanding of their own life paths.

Oya's narrative teaches the importance of grounding oneself in reality while remaining open to personal growth and connection. Practices such as storytelling, ritualistic engagement with elements of nature, and community involvement can help individuals align with Oya's energy. Emulating her resilience and empathy, individuals can navigate their own life's trials with a balanced and empowered outlook.

THE ORPHAN/EVERYMAN

In sum, Oya's stories and attributes exemplify the Orphan/Everyman archetype's essence. Her experiences of love, conflict, betrayal, and empowerment offer profound insights into the human condition, making her an enduring source of inspiration and strength for those who seek to connect with the universal themes of resilience and community.

EXERCISES & RITUALS

Aligning with Oya and the Orphan/Everyman archetype involves practices that promote resilience, empathy, and personal transformation. These rituals and exercises are designed to help individuals overcome adversity and the shadow aspects of feeling victimized or isolated, fostering mental health and well-being.

Fire Cleansing Ritual

Supplies Needed:
- A fire-safe bowl or cauldron, paper, pen, matches or a lighter.

Guidelines:
1. Write down any feelings of victimization, past traumas, or current adversities you are facing on pieces of paper.
2. Set up a safe space for a small fire, using a fire-safe bowl or cauldron.
3. Light the papers on fire, one by one, as you focus on releasing these negative emotions. Visualize Oya's powerful winds carrying away the ashes, symbolizing your release from these burdens.
4. As the fire burns, recite affirmations of strength and resilience, invoking Oya's transformative energy to empower you.

Benefits:
This fire cleansing ritual is a symbolic way to let go of negativity and embrace personal transformation. It aligns with Oya's association with fire and storms, promoting mental clarity and emotional resilience.

Wind Whisper Ritual

Supplies Needed:
- A quiet outdoor space with a gentle breeze, a scarf or ribbon.

Guidelines:
1. Find a peaceful spot outdoors where you can feel the wind. Bring a scarf or ribbon with you.
2. Hold the scarf or ribbon in the wind, allowing it to flow freely. As it moves, speak your intentions or challenges into the wind, asking for Oya's guidance and support.
3. Visualize the wind carrying your words and transforming your struggles into strength and resilience.
4. After a few minutes, tie the scarf or ribbon around your wrist or place it in a meaningful location as a reminder of Oya's presence and support.

Benefits:
This ritual connects you with Oya's element of wind, promoting a sense of release and renewal. It helps in transforming negative emotions into positive actions and resilience.

Transformative Dance Ritual

Supplies Needed:
- Comfortable clothing, a private space, music that inspires strength and transformation.

Guidelines:
1. Dress comfortably and find a private space where you can move freely.

2. Play music that evokes a sense of strength, transformation, and empowerment. This could be drumming, rhythmic beats, or any music that resonates with Oya's energy.
3. Begin to dance, allowing your body to move freely and expressively. Focus on releasing any pent-up emotions or stresses through your movements.
4. As you dance, visualize Oya's energy flowing through you, transforming your struggles into strength and resilience.

Benefits:
Dance is a powerful way to connect with Oya's transformative energy. It promotes physical and emotional release, helping to overcome feelings of victimization and fostering a sense of empowerment and resilience.

Ancestor Connection Ritual

Supplies Needed:
- A candle, a photo or memento of an ancestor, a small bowl of water.

Guidelines:
1. Light a candle and place it next to a photo or memento of an ancestor who inspires you.
2. Fill a small bowl with water and place it next to the candle.
3. Sit quietly and reflect on the strength and resilience of your ancestors. Visualize their struggles and triumphs, drawing inspiration from their journeys.
4. Dip your fingers into the water and touch your forehead, asking for the wisdom and strength of your ancestors to help you overcome your challenges.
5. Spend a few minutes in silent reflection, thanking your ancestors and Oya for their guidance and support.

Benefits:
This ritual connects you with your lineage and the resilience of your ancestors. It aligns with Oya's role as a guardian of the dead, promoting a sense of continuity, strength, and support.

By engaging in these exercises and rituals, individuals can align themselves with Oya and the Orphan/Everyman archetype. These practices not only help in overcoming the shadow sides of feeling victimized or isolated but also foster a sense of resilience, empathy, and transformation, promoting overall mental health and well-being.

REFLECTIONS

Oya's deep and multifaceted narrative in Yoruba mythology offers a unique perspective on the Orphan/Everyman archetype. As the orisha of winds, storms, and transformation, Oya exemplifies the resilience and adaptability central to this archetype. Her life's stories, filled with trials, transitions, and triumphs, shed light on the universal struggle for belonging and identity that defines the Orphan/Everyman.

Oya's experiences of loss and change, particularly her transitions from one realm to another and her role as a guardian of the cemetery, resonate with the Orphan/Everyman's journey through adversity. Her ability to navigate these transformations while maintaining her strength and purpose exemplifies the Orphan/Everyman's capacity to endure and adapt. Oya teaches that true strength often comes from facing life's storms and using those challenges as catalysts for growth and transformation.

Moreover, Oya's role in Yoruba mythology highlights the archetype's potential for empowerment and leadership. Despite the hardships and isolation often associated with the Orphan/Everyman, Oya rises to become a powerful figure who commands respect and wields significant influence over both earthly and spiritual realms. Her story is a testament to the

THE ORPHAN/EVERYMAN

potential within every individual to overcome adversity and to assert control over their destiny.

Oya's narrative invites those who see themselves in the Orphan/Everyman archetype to recognize their own potential for resilience and transformation. It encourages embracing the winds of change as opportunities for personal growth and renewal. Her journey underscores the importance of staying true to oneself, forging a unique path, and using one's experiences of adversity as a foundation for empowerment and leadership.

Let Oya's story inspire those aligned with the Orphan/Everyman archetype to move beyond mere survival, to thrive and to lead. Let her resilience remind us that our greatest trials can forge our most profound strengths, and that each of us holds the power to redefine our path and impact the world around us.

Chapter 5

The Hero

The Hero archetype is one of the most universally recognized and celebrated figures in mythology and psychology. Representing the qualities of courage, strength, and determination, the Hero embodies the drive to overcome obstacles, achieve greatness, and make a significant impact on the world. This archetype is characterized by a willingness to confront danger, a relentless pursuit of goals, and an unwavering belief in one's ability to triumph against all odds.

In many cultures, the Hero is depicted as a figure who embarks on a journey, faces trials and tribulations, and ultimately achieves a transformative victory. This journey, often referred to as the Hero's Journey, is a central motif in the works of mythologist Joseph Campbell, who identified common patterns and stages in the stories of heroes across different cultures. The Hero's Journey typically involves a call to adventure, crossing thresholds, facing challenges, achieving a climactic victory, and returning home transformed.

The qualities of the Hero are not limited to physical strength and bravery but also encompass moral and psychological courage. Heroes often face inner demons and moral dilemmas, requiring them to make difficult choices that test their integrity and resolve. This aspect of the Hero archetype highlights the importance of inner strength and the ability to remain true to one's values in the face of adversity.

Strengths and Weaknesses
The Hero archetype is a powerful symbol of bravery and perseverance, inspiring individuals to pursue their dreams and overcome obstacles. The strengths of the Hero include a strong sense of purpose, the ability to inspire others, and a resilient spirit that refuses to give up. These qualities make the Hero a compelling figure who can lead others through challenging times and achieve remarkable feats.

However, the Hero's strengths can also become weaknesses if not balanced properly. Bravery can turn into recklessness, and determination can become stubbornness. One of the significant pitfalls of the Hero archetype is the potential for arrogance and hubris. Heroes who become overly confident in their abilities may underestimate the challenges they face or disregard the contributions and wisdom of others. This arrogance can lead to downfall or failure, as seen in many mythological and literary examples where heroes meet tragic ends due to their hubris.

The dual nature of the Hero's traits underscores the importance of humility and self-awareness. True heroism involves recognizing one's limitations, valuing the support and guidance of others, and understanding that strength comes from collaboration and mutual respect.

Cultural Examples
The Hero archetype is deeply embedded in the cultural fabric of societies worldwide, manifesting in various forms across literature, film, and mythology. One of the most famous literary examples of the Hero is

Homer's *Odysseus*, whose epic journey in *The Odyssey* epitomizes the trials and triumphs of the Hero's Journey. Odysseus's courage, intelligence, and determination enable him to overcome numerous obstacles and ultimately return home to Ithaca.

In modern literature, the Hero archetype can be seen in characters such as J.K. Rowling's *Harry Potter*, who faces extraordinary challenges and grows into a powerful and wise leader. Harry's journey from a young, inexperienced boy to a heroic figure who defeats the dark forces of Voldemort exemplifies the transformative power of the Hero's Journey.

In film, the Hero archetype is vividly portrayed in characters like *Luke Skywalker* from the *Star Wars* saga. Luke's journey from a farm boy on Tatooine to a Jedi Knight who confronts and redeems his father, Darth Vader, is a classic example of the Hero's Journey. His courage, resilience, and moral fortitude inspire audiences and underscore the timeless appeal of the Hero archetype.

Mythological examples abound, with figures like *Hercules*, *King Arthur*, and *Beowulf* embodying the Hero archetype in different cultural contexts. These heroes undertake perilous quests, face formidable foes, and achieve great deeds that cement their legacy in the collective consciousness.

In today's world, the Hero archetype also manifests in the form of social activists and leaders who challenge the status quo and fight for justice. Figures like Malala Yousafzai, who advocates for girls' education worldwide, or Greta Thunberg, who leads the charge against climate change, exemplify the modern Hero's role in society. These individuals take on significant personal risks to pursue their missions, embodying the Hero's willingness to sacrifice for a cause greater than themselves.

Historical or Contemporary Figures
Martin Luther King Jr. (1929–1968)
Dr. Martin Luther King Jr., the leader of the American civil rights movement, is another powerful example of the Hero archetype. Through his leadership, nonviolent protests, and powerful oratory, King fought against racial segregation and injustice. His vision of equality and his willingness to risk his life for the cause exemplify the Hero's journey, marked by courage, sacrifice, and the pursuit of a higher purpose.

Winston Churchill (1874–1965)
Winston Churchill, the British Prime Minister during World War II, is celebrated for his leadership and resilience during one of history's most challenging periods. His determination to stand against Nazi Germany, especially during the darkest days of the war when Britain faced the threat of invasion, exemplifies the Hero archetype.

Churchill's speeches, marked by their defiant optimism and rallying cry for perseverance, inspired not only the British people but also the world. His ability to navigate the complexities of war, maintain morale, and ultimately lead the Allies to victory demonstrates the courage, strength, and resolve associated with the Hero archetype. Churchill's legacy as a wartime leader and his role in shaping the course of the 20th century make him a fitting example of the Hero archetype in modern history.

In Psychology
The Hero archetype is also relevant in the field of psychology, where it represents the process of individuation and personal growth. Jungian therapists often explore the Hero's journey as a metaphor for the client's path towards self-discovery, encouraging them to face their inner demons and emerge stronger. The Hero's journey is a powerful framework for understanding the challenges and triumphs of human life, making it a central theme in both personal development and collective narratives.

Shadow Side

While the Hero archetype is often celebrated for its positive qualities, it also has a shadow side that can manifest negatively. One of the primary negative aspects of the Hero is the potential for hubris, or excessive pride. Heroes who become too confident in their abilities may disregard warnings, take unnecessary risks, and alienate those around them. This arrogance can lead to tragic outcomes, as seen in the stories of heroes like *Icarus*, whose overconfidence led to his downfall.

Another negative manifestation of the Hero archetype is the tendency to become overly focused on external achievements at the expense of personal relationships and inner growth. Heroes who prioritize their quests and victories over their emotional well-being and connections with others may end up isolated and unfulfilled. This imbalance can result in a sense of emptiness and a lack of genuine happiness, despite external successes.

The Hero's relentless drive to overcome obstacles and achieve goals can also lead to burnout and exhaustion. The constant pressure to perform and succeed may take a toll on the Hero's mental and physical health, leading to stress and a diminished quality of life. Recognizing and addressing these potential pitfalls is crucial for maintaining a healthy and balanced approach to the Hero's journey.

Path to Individuation

The path to individuation, as described by Carl Jung, involves integrating various aspects of the self to achieve wholeness and self-realization. For individuals embodying the Hero archetype, this process requires balancing the positive qualities of courage and determination with humility, self-awareness, and emotional intelligence.

One way to achieve this balance is through self-reflection and mindfulness practices. Heroes can benefit from regularly assessing their motivations, strengths, and weaknesses, ensuring that their actions align with their core values and long-term goals. Mindfulness meditation, journaling, and seeking feedback from trusted mentors can help heroes stay grounded and connected to their inner selves.

Building and maintaining strong personal relationships is also essential for balancing the Hero archetype. Heroes should cultivate meaningful connections with family, friends, and communities, valuing the support and wisdom of others. These relationships provide emotional sustenance and remind the Hero that true strength comes from collaboration and mutual respect.

Another crucial aspect of the Hero's path to individuation is embracing vulnerability and acknowledging limitations. Heroes should recognize that asking for help and admitting weaknesses does not diminish their strength but rather enhances it. Embracing vulnerability fosters resilience and allows the Hero to grow and learn from challenges.

Finally, engaging in regular self-care practices is vital for preventing burnout and maintaining overall well-being. Heroes should prioritize physical health through exercise, nutrition, and adequate rest, as well as mental health through relaxation techniques, hobbies, and creative expression. These practices ensure that the Hero remains physically and emotionally capable of facing challenges and achieving goals.

In conclusion, the Hero archetype represents a powerful and inspiring figure characterized by courage, strength, and determination. By understanding and integrating the positive and negative aspects of this archetype, individuals can embark on their Hero's Journey with balance, humility, and self-awareness, ultimately achieving personal growth and self-realization.

THE HERO

SHANGO AS THE HERO

In the pantheon of Yoruba orisha, Shango stands out as a quintessential embodiment of the Hero archetype. Revered as the god of thunder, lightning, and fire, Shango is known for his immense strength, courage, and dynamic presence. His stories and attributes align closely with the qualities of the Hero archetype, making him a powerful symbol of bravery, resilience, and transformative power. Celebrated for his formidable abilities and leadership qualities, Shango's heroism is marked by remarkable feats and victories in battle. However, Shango's heroism is multifaceted, encompassing not only his valor and triumphs but also his vanity, impulsiveness, and the consequences of his actions.

Shango's mythological narratives are rich with examples of heroic feats and trials that mirror the Hero's Journey. One of the most well-known stories involves Shango's rise to power as a king and his subsequent fall due to hubris. As a king, Shango was a fierce and just ruler, known for his formidable combat skills and his ability to command thunder and lightning. However, his overconfidence and desire for absolute power led to his downfall, a classic example of the Hero's shadow side manifesting as hubris.

Despite his fall, Shango's legacy endured, and he was deified as an orisha, continuing to inspire and empower his followers. This narrative highlights the transformative power of the Hero's journey, where even in failure, there is the potential for redemption and spiritual elevation. Shango's story serves as a reminder that true heroism involves not just triumphs but also the ability to learn and grow from setbacks.

Engaging with Shango's energy can provide individuals with the courage and determination to face their own challenges. Through rituals, invocations, and offerings, devotees can connect with Shango's dynamic power and invoke his qualities of strength and resilience. Common offerings to Shango include red wine, roosters, and spicy foods, reflecting his fiery nature.

Drumming and dancing are also central to Shango's worship, embodying his vibrant and energetic spirit.

Strengths and Weaknesses
Shango's primary strengths are his unparalleled bravery, physical prowess, and leadership skills. He is often depicted wielding a double-headed axe, symbolizing his might and authority. Shango's strength is not just physical but also spiritual; his command over thunder and lightning demonstrates his powerful connection to the natural and supernatural realms.

However, Shango's weaknesses include his vanity and impetuosity. His desire for recognition and admiration often leads to reckless decisions, showcasing the shadow side of the Hero archetype. These traits sometimes result in dire consequences, underscoring the need for balance and humility in true heroism.

Shadow Side
The shadow side of Shango's Hero archetype is evident in his vanity, impulsiveness, and susceptibility to flattery. His need for constant admiration and validation often leads him to make hasty decisions without considering the consequences. This aspect of his personality sometimes results in conflicts and challenges that could have been avoided with more foresight and humility.

For instance, Shango's rivalry with Ogun and his exchange with Orunmila both highlight his tendency to act on impulse rather than reason. His competitive nature with Ogun led to unnecessary strife, while his deal with Orunmila, though it enhanced his public image, deprived him of valuable foresight and wisdom. These stories serve as cautionary tales about the dangers of unchecked ego and the importance of maintaining a balanced perspective.

Path to Individuation

Balancing and integrating the Hero archetype involves acknowledging and embracing one's strengths while also recognizing and addressing one's weaknesses. For Shango, this means channeling his courage, strength, and leadership qualities in positive and constructive ways. It also involves cultivating humility, patience, and the wisdom to make thoughtful decisions.

Engaging with Shango's energy through rituals and personal reflection can help individuals tap into their inner heroism while also confronting and integrating their shadow aspects. Practices such as meditation, martial arts, and dance can serve as powerful tools for connecting with Shango's dynamic energy and achieving personal growth.

The Legacy of Shango in Cultural Contexts

Shango's influence extends beyond Yoruba mythology into various cultural and religious practices in the African diaspora. In religions such as Santería and Candomblé, Shango is revered as a powerful orisha who embodies the Hero archetype. His attributes of strength, courage, and justice continue to resonate with individuals seeking empowerment and guidance in their lives.

In Santería, Shango is often syncretized with St. Barbara, reflecting the blending of Yoruba and Catholic traditions. Devotees celebrate his feast day with vibrant ceremonies that include drumming, dancing, and offerings. These practices underscore Shango's enduring relevance as a symbol of heroism and resilience.

In popular culture, Shango's image and stories have inspired numerous artistic and literary works. His dynamic presence and heroic qualities make him a compelling figure in literature, music, and visual arts. By engaging with Shango's archetypal energy, artists and creators can tap into a wellspring of inspiration and creative power.

SHANGO STORIES

Shango's heroism and complex character are vividly portrayed in various Yoruba myths and cultural expressions. Two notable stories highlight his interactions with other orisha, illustrating his virtues and flaws.

Rivalry with Ogun
Shango's rivalry with Ogun, the god of iron and war, is one of the most famous tales in Yoruba mythology. Ogun, known for his craftsmanship and martial prowess, often found himself at odds with Shango. Their rivalry stemmed from their contrasting domains and personalities—Shango's flamboyant and aggressive nature clashed with Ogun's more methodical and disciplined approach.

The story goes that Shango and Ogun competed for supremacy, each trying to outdo the other in feats of strength and bravery. In one account, Shango challenged Ogun to a contest to determine who was the greatest warrior. Despite Shango's impressive skills, Ogun's strategic mind and unyielding determination often gave him the upper hand. This rivalry highlights Shango's competitive spirit and his struggles with jealousy and pride. It also underscores the importance of respecting the strengths and contributions of others, a lesson that Shango had to learn through his repeated confrontations with Ogun.

Exchange with Orunmila
Another significant story involves Shango's exchange of his gifts of divination with Orunmila, the orisha of wisdom and divination, for the ability to dance. Orunmila was known for his deep insight and foresight, qualities that Shango admired but did not possess. Desiring to enhance his charismatic appeal and command over his followers, Shango approached Orunmila with a proposition.

THE HERO

In exchange for the ability to dance with unmatched grace and rhythm, Shango gave up his divinatory powers to Orunmila. This exchange made Shango an even more captivating figure, as his dances during rituals and celebrations became legendary. However, it also meant that he lost a valuable aspect of his spiritual toolkit, which had helped him foresee and navigate challenges. This story illustrates Shango's vanity and desire for immediate gratification, as well as the long-term repercussions of sacrificing inner wisdom for external allure.

EXERCISES & RITUALS

Aligning oneself with Shango, the orisha of thunder, lightning, and fire, can be a transformative experience that cultivates courage, strength, and leadership qualities. Here are some detailed exercises and rituals to help individuals connect with Shango and the Hero archetype while addressing the shadow side of impulsiveness and recklessness.

Fire Meditation and Visualization

Supplies Needed:
- Candle, matches or lighter, comfortable seating.

Guidelines:
1. Preparation: Find a quiet space where you won't be disturbed. Sit comfortably with a candle placed safely in front of you.
2. Lighting the Candle: Light the candle, focusing on the flame. As you do so, call upon Shango, asking for his presence and guidance.
3. Meditation: Close your eyes and take deep breaths. Visualize Shango's fiery energy enveloping you, filling you with courage and strength.
4. Visualization Exercise: Imagine a scenario where you face a fear or challenge. See yourself confronting it with the bravery and

confidence of Shango. Visualize the successful outcome of your actions.
5. Reflection: After 10-15 minutes, open your eyes and extinguish the candle. Reflect on the experience and jot down any insights or feelings in a journal.

Explanation:
This meditation helps individuals harness Shango's fiery energy, promoting courage and resilience. The visualization exercise allows one to mentally practice overcoming fears and challenges, strengthening their resolve in real-life situations.

Thunderstorm Ritual

Supplies Needed:
- None (conducted during a thunderstorm).

Guidelines:
1. Timing: Perform this ritual during an actual thunderstorm to connect deeply with Shango's natural element.
2. Outdoor Experience: Find a safe, sheltered outdoor spot where you can experience the storm without risk. Alternatively, sit near an open window where you can hear and see the storm.
3. Invocation: Close your eyes and breathe deeply. Listen to the thunder and feel the energy of the storm. Call upon Shango, asking for his guidance and strength.
4. Affirmations: As the storm rages, speak affirmations aloud, such as "I am strong," "I am courageous," "I face challenges with confidence."
5. Gratitude: Once the storm subsides, thank Shango for his presence and guidance. Reflect on how the storm made you feel and any emotions or thoughts it brought up.

THE HERO

<u>Explanation</u>:
Thunderstorms are powerful natural events that embody Shango's energy. This ritual allows individuals to draw strength and courage from the storm, fostering a sense of empowerment and fearlessness.

Warrior Dance

<u>Supplies Needed</u>:
- Drumming music (recorded or live), a space to move freely.

<u>Guidelines</u>:
1. Preparation: Choose a space where you can move freely and won't be disturbed. Play rhythmic drumming music that evokes a sense of power and energy.
2. Invocation: Before starting, invoke Shango by calling his name and asking for his guidance. Feel his presence as you prepare to dance.
3. Dance: Begin to move to the rhythm of the drums. Let your movements be strong and powerful, embodying the warrior spirit of Shango. Imagine yourself as a warrior, facing and overcoming obstacles.
4. Focus: As you dance, focus on releasing any fears or doubts. Allow the energy of the dance to fill you with confidence and strength.
5. Closing: After dancing for 10-20 minutes, gradually slow your movements and come to a stop. Thank Shango for his guidance and reflect on the experience.

<u>Explanation</u>:
The Warrior Dance is a physical expression of Shango's energy, helping individuals embody the qualities of strength, courage, and resilience. It also serves as a way to release fears and doubts, fostering a sense of empowerment.

Symbolic Offering to Shango

<u>Supplies Needed</u>:
- Red cloth, small axe or metal symbol (can be a miniature), fruits (such as bananas or apples), and a safe outdoor space.

<u>Guidelines</u>:
1. Preparation: In a safe outdoor space, lay down the red cloth as an altar. Place the small axe or metal symbol and the fruits on the cloth.
2. Invocation: Call upon Shango, asking for his presence and guidance. Explain that the offering is a symbol of your commitment to embodying the Hero archetype.
3. Offering: Arrange the fruits around the axe or metal symbol, speaking your intentions aloud. Ask Shango to help you cultivate courage, strength, and wise leadership.
4. Meditation: Sit quietly in front of the altar, meditating on Shango's qualities and how you can embody them in your life. Visualize yourself overcoming fears and challenges with his strength.
5. Closing: Thank Shango for his presence and guidance. Leave the offering in place for a while before respectfully disposing of it.

<u>Explanation</u>:
This symbolic offering ritual connects individuals to Shango's energy, reinforcing their commitment to developing the Hero archetype's qualities. The act of offering and meditation helps internalize these traits, fostering personal growth and empowerment.

By engaging in these exercises and rituals, individuals can align themselves with Shango and the Hero archetype, cultivating courage, strength, and resilience while addressing the shadow side of impulsiveness and recklessness. These practices provide a holistic approach to personal development, integrating physical, mental, and spiritual elements to promote overall well-being.

THE HERO

REFLECTIONS

Shango's dynamic presence within Yoruba mythology and his embodiment of the Hero archetype resonate deeply through the tales of his courage, leadership, and consequential actions. His narrative, marked by dramatic feats and passionate encounters, provides a compelling illustration of what it means to be a hero in both ancient and modern contexts.

As the orisha of thunder, lightning, and fire, Shango symbolizes the raw power and charisma typical of heroic figures. His stories of battles won and justice delivered showcase the traditional attributes of the Hero—bravery, strength, and the drive to overcome adversity. Yet, Shango's tales also delve into the complexities of heroism, revealing the burdens that often accompany great power and responsibility.

Shango's journey through triumphs and trials highlights the dual nature of the Hero archetype. His capacity to lead and inspire is as significant as his moments of fallibility, where his fiery temper leads to unintended consequences. These aspects of his character invite us to consider the Hero not merely as a figure of unblemished valor but as a nuanced being, whose flaws and strengths are intrinsically linked.

Shango's narrative encourages those who identify with the Hero archetype to embrace their potential for leadership while remaining vigilant of the ethical dimensions of their actions. The tales of Shango teach that true heroism involves not only the might to change the world but also the wisdom to guide those changes judiciously. They remind us that every hero's journey includes learning from missteps and striving towards a balance between power and responsibility.

Therefore, let us draw inspiration from Shango's legacy to approach our challenges with courage and a readiness to act for the greater good. Let his stories inspire us to lead with both strength and compassion, to seek justice with consideration, and to wield our influence thoughtfully. By embodying the balanced Hero, we can aspire to make impactful changes in our lives and in the lives of others, ensuring that our actions lead to outcomes that are as honorable as the intentions behind them.

Chapter 6

The Caregiver

The Caregiver archetype is characterized by an innate desire to nurture and protect others. Individuals embodying this archetype are often empathetic, compassionate, and selfless, prioritizing the needs and well-being of others above their own. This archetype is deeply rooted in the ideals of altruism, kindness, and a sense of duty towards the care and support of others. Caregivers often find fulfillment in acts of service and derive satisfaction from seeing others thrive and succeed. Their nurturing nature makes them excellent providers of emotional support and practical assistance, often serving as the backbone of their communities and families.

Caregivers excel in creating safe and supportive environments where others can grow and develop. They are often seen as reliable and trustworthy, offering a comforting presence in times of need. Their strength lies in their ability to understand and respond to the emotional and physical needs of others, making them indispensable in roles that require caregiving, such as parenting, teaching, nursing, and counseling. However, the intense focus on others can sometimes lead to neglect of their own needs, making self-care an essential aspect of maintaining their well-being.

Strengths and Weaknesses

The primary strength of the Caregiver lies in their altruism. Their selfless dedication to the well-being of others is driven by a genuine desire to help and support, often going to great lengths to ensure the comfort and safety of those around them. Another significant strength is their empathy. Caregivers possess a deep sense of empathy, which allows them to understand and connect with the emotions and needs of others. This quality makes them excellent listeners and compassionate companions. Additionally, caregivers are known for their reliability. They provide a stable and secure presence, offering consistent support and care.

However, the shadow side of the Caregiver archetype can manifest as martyrdom. Caregivers may neglect their own needs and well-being, leading to burnout and resentment. Their selflessness can become a form of self-sacrifice that is detrimental to their own health and happiness. Another potential weakness is overprotectiveness. Caregivers may become overly protective, stifling the independence and growth of those they care for. Their desire to shield others from harm can result in a lack of autonomy for those they seek to help. Additionally, caregivers often struggle with feelings of guilt. They may feel guilty for not being able to help everyone or for taking time for themselves, leading to a perpetual cycle of overexertion and self-neglect.

Cultural Examples

The Caregiver archetype is prevalent in various cultural narratives, literature, film, and mythology. In Louisa May Alcott's *Little Women*, the character of Marmee exemplifies the Caregiver archetype through her nurturing and selfless care for her daughters and the community. In the movie *Forrest Gump*, the character of Mrs. Gump, Forrest's mother, represents the Caregiver archetype with her unwavering support and guidance for her son. In Greek mythology, Demeter, the goddess of agriculture and the harvest, embodies the Caregiver archetype through her role as a nurturing mother who ensures the fertility of the earth and the well-being of humanity.

THE CAREGIVER

The Caregiver archetype also remains a significant force in contemporary society, particularly in the context of caregiving professions and roles that prioritize nurturing, protection, and compassion. This archetype is strongly represented in the healthcare industry, where doctors, nurses, and therapists embody the Caregiver's commitment to the well-being of others. The global response to the COVID-19 pandemic has further highlighted the importance of the Caregiver archetype, as healthcare workers have been celebrated as heroes for their selfless dedication to saving lives.

In popular culture, the Caregiver archetype is often portrayed through characters who provide emotional support and guidance to others. For example, in the television series *This Is Us*, the character of Rebecca Pearson exemplifies the Caregiver through her role as a devoted mother who nurtures and protects her children through various challenges. This archetype's presence in media serves as a reminder of the importance of compassion and empathy in building strong, supportive relationships.

Historical or Contemporary Figures
Mother Teresa (1910–1997)
Mother Teresa, founder of the Missionaries of Charity, dedicated her life to serving the poor, sick, and dying. Her work in the slums of Calcutta and her unwavering commitment to the most vulnerable exemplify the Caregiver archetype. Mother Teresa's life was a testament to selfless love and compassion, embodying the Caregiver's deep desire to alleviate suffering and nurture others.

Florence Nightingale (1820–1910)
Florence Nightingale, known as the founder of modern nursing, also represents the Caregiver archetype. During the Crimean War, Nightingale's pioneering work in battlefield hospitals revolutionized medical care. Her focus on sanitation, patient care, and compassionate service has left an enduring legacy in the field of nursing and healthcare.

In Psychology
The Caregiver archetype is also relevant in contemporary discussions about mental health and self-care. As society becomes increasingly aware of the importance of mental and emotional well-being, the Caregiver's emphasis on nurturing oneself and others has taken on new significance. Practices such as mindfulness, therapy, and community support systems reflect the Caregiver's influence, encouraging individuals to prioritize their own health while also caring for those around them. This balance between self-care and caregiving is essential in today's fast-paced, often stressful world.

Shadow Side
The shadow side of the Caregiver archetype can manifest in several ways. Caregivers may neglect their own needs and well-being, leading to burnout and resentment. Their selflessness can become a form of self-sacrifice that is detrimental to their own health and happiness. Overprotectiveness is another potential negative manifestation. Caregivers may become overly protective, stifling the independence and growth of those they care for. Their desire to shield others from harm can result in a lack of autonomy for those they seek to help. Additionally, caregivers often struggle with feelings of guilt. They may feel guilty for not being able to help everyone or for taking time for themselves, leading to a perpetual cycle of overexertion and self-neglect.

Path to Individuation
To achieve individuation, individuals must learn to balance and integrate the Caregiver archetype. This process involves recognizing the importance of self-care and setting healthy boundaries to avoid burnout and resentment. Caregivers must acknowledge their own needs and well-being, understanding that they cannot effectively care for others if they are not also caring for themselves. Developing a sense of autonomy and allowing others to develop their own independence is also crucial. By fostering independence in those they care for, caregivers can avoid becoming

overprotective and stifling growth. Additionally, caregivers must learn to manage feelings of guilt and understand that taking time for themselves is not selfish but necessary for their overall well-being. By achieving this balance, individuals can harness the positive aspects of the Caregiver archetype while mitigating its potential negative manifestations.

YEMAYA AS THE CAREGIVER

Yemaya, the Yoruba orisha of the ocean and motherhood, epitomizes the Caregiver archetype. She is revered as a powerful maternal figure, embodying the nurturing and protective qualities associated with this archetype. Yemaya is often depicted as a nurturing mother who cares deeply for her children, offering them guidance, protection, and unconditional love. Her connection to the ocean, a symbol of life and sustenance, underscores her role as a life-giver and sustainer. Yemaya's presence is calming and reassuring, much like the gentle ebb and flow of the sea.

In Yoruba mythology, Yemaya is celebrated for her ability to provide comfort and healing. She is often invoked in times of distress, with her followers turning to her for solace and support. Her nurturing spirit is evident in the various myths that highlight her protective nature. One such story describes how Yemaya transformed into a river to save her children from danger, illustrating her willingness to go to great lengths to ensure their safety. This act of self-sacrifice and protection underscores her deep commitment to the well-being of her followers (Olmos and Paravisini-Gebert, 2003).

Strengths and Weaknesses
Yemaya's strengths as a Caregiver are evident in her boundless compassion and protective instincts. She is celebrated for her ability to provide emotional support and physical protection, often using her powers to shield her children from harm. Her empathy allows her to connect deeply with those in need, offering comfort and reassurance in times of crisis. Yemaya's

nurturing nature is not limited to her human children; she is also seen as a protector of all living beings, reflecting her expansive and inclusive sense of care.

However, Yemaya's intense protectiveness can also be a double-edged sword. While her desire to shield her loved ones from harm is commendable, it can sometimes lead to overprotectiveness. This can stifle the growth and independence of those she cares for, preventing them from developing their own strengths and resilience. Furthermore, Yemaya's immense empathy can result in emotional exhaustion, as she absorbs the burdens and sorrows of those around her. This highlights the importance of balance in caregiving, where the caregiver must also attend to their own needs to sustain their ability to care for others.

Cultural Examples
Yemaya's influence is profound and widespread, extending beyond Yoruba mythology into various cultural practices and belief systems. In Afro-Caribbean religions such as Santería and Candomblé, Yemaya is venerated as a powerful mother figure who provides comfort, protection, and guidance to her devotees. Her worship involves elaborate rituals and offerings, often conducted near bodies of water, reflecting her connection to the ocean and her nurturing spirit. These rituals include offerings of fruits, flowers, and shells, which are believed to please Yemaya and invoke her blessings.

Yemaya's cultural significance is also evident in the arts. In literature, she is often portrayed as a nurturing and protective figure, symbolizing the universal themes of motherhood and care. In music, songs dedicated to Yemaya celebrate her nurturing qualities and her role as a protector. Visual arts often depict Yemaya as a serene and maternal figure, surrounded by symbols of the sea and life. These cultural representations reinforce Yemaya's role as the ultimate caregiver, embodying the ideals of compassion, protection, and unconditional love.

THE CAREGIVER

Shadow Side

The shadow side of Yemaya's Caregiver archetype includes the potential for self-neglect and martyrdom. Yemaya's intense focus on the well-being of others can lead her to neglect her own needs and health. This self-sacrificial behavior, while noble, can result in physical and emotional burnout. Additionally, her overprotectiveness can become a hindrance, preventing her children and followers from learning valuable lessons through their own experiences. This aspect of the shadow side underscores the importance of balance in caregiving, emphasizing that nurturing must also include self-care and the promotion of independence in others.

The shadow side of Yemaya's Caregiver archetype also includes the potential for dependency. Her intense desire to protect and care for others can lead to creating a dynamic where her loved ones become overly reliant on her, unable to develop their own strengths and independence. This can stifle their growth and prevent them from experiencing the challenges necessary for personal development. Additionally, Yemaya's deep emotional connection with those she cares for can sometimes lead to emotional entanglement, where she takes on their pain and suffering to the detriment of her own well-being.

Path to Individuation

Achieving individuation with the Caregiver archetype involves balancing selflessness with self-care. Yemaya's path to individuation requires recognizing the importance of maintaining her own well-being while continuing to provide care and support to others. This balance can be achieved through rituals that emphasize self-renewal and boundary-setting. Engaging in water-based purification rituals, such as cleansing baths or offerings to the ocean, can help Yemaya cleanse herself of accumulated emotional burdens and rejuvenate her spirit. Additionally, setting healthy boundaries with those she cares for can prevent the development of unhealthy dependencies and encourage autonomy and resilience in her followers.

One practical approach to achieving this balance is the practice of self-care rituals. For Yemaya, these rituals can involve spending time near water, meditating by the sea, or taking cleansing baths with sea salt and herbs. These practices can help her release the emotional burdens she carries and recharge her energies. Another important aspect of individuation is learning to set healthy boundaries. Yemaya can achieve this by encouraging her loved ones to take responsibility for their own lives, offering guidance and support without taking over their challenges.

Furthermore, Yemaya can integrate her caregiving nature by fostering resilience in those she cares for. This involves teaching them the skills and providing the tools they need to navigate their own challenges. By empowering others, Yemaya can ensure that her nurturing efforts lead to the growth and independence of those she cares for, creating a more balanced and sustainable caregiving dynamic. This balanced approach allows her to continue providing compassionate care without sacrificing her own well-being, embodying the ideal of nurturing in its most holistic form.

YEMAYA STORIES

Yemaya, the revered Yoruba orisha of the ocean, is often celebrated as a quintessential mother figure in the pantheon of orishas. Her nurturing and protective nature is exemplified through various myths and stories that highlight her role as the giver of life and caretaker of the orishas. In these tales, Yemaya's capacity for love and care extends beyond her biological children, illustrating her profound commitment to the well-being of all orishas under her watch.

Birth and Care of the Orishas
One of the most well-known stories about Yemaya centers on her role as the progenitor of the orishas. According to Yoruba mythology, Yemaya gave birth to a multitude of orishas, each representing different aspects of nature

and human life. This act of creation underscores her position as a life-giver and emphasizes her deep connection to the ocean, a symbol of fertility and sustenance. Yemaya's ability to bring forth life from the depths of the sea highlights her immense power and nurturing essence (Olmos and Paravisini-Gebert, 2003).

In addition to her biological children, Yemaya is also known for raising orishas who were not her own. Among these are Shango and the Ibeji. Shango, the orisha of thunder, lightning, and fire, is one of the most prominent figures in Yoruba mythology. Though not born to Yemaya, Shango was raised by her, benefiting from her wisdom, protection, and nurturing care. Yemaya's influence is evident in Shango's formidable strength and dynamic personality, traits that reflect her own powerful nature.

The Ibeji, the twin orishas of joy and abundance, are also said to have been raised by Yemaya. The story of the Ibeji highlights Yemaya's ability to nurture and guide young orishas, ensuring their growth and development. Under her care, the Ibeji thrived, becoming symbols of harmony and prosperity. Yemaya's role in their upbringing underscores her dedication to fostering the well-being of those in her care, regardless of their origins.

Successes and Failures

Yemaya's successes as a caregiver are manifold, illustrated by the thriving lives of the orishas she nurtured. Her ability to provide love, guidance, and protection ensured that the orishas under her care grew to embody the qualities and powers they are known for. Shango, for instance, became a formidable warrior and leader, his strength and courage a testament to Yemaya's influence. The Ibeji, embodying joy and abundance, also reflect the nurturing environment Yemaya provided, one that allowed them to flourish and spread positivity.

However, Yemaya's journey as a caregiver is not without its challenges and failures. Her deep emotional connections and protective instincts sometimes led to overprotectiveness, potentially stifling the independence of the orishas she cared for. This overprotectiveness could result in conflicts and misunderstandings, as seen in some myths where the orishas sought to assert their independence. Additionally, Yemaya's intense emotional involvement often left her vulnerable to emotional exhaustion, highlighting the inherent challenges in balancing self-care with caregiving.

One notable story that illustrates both Yemaya's successes and challenges is her relationship with Shango. While she successfully nurtured him into a powerful orisha, their dynamic was not without tension. Shango's fiery temperament and desire for independence sometimes clashed with Yemaya's protective nature. This tension underscores the delicate balance caregivers must maintain between providing support and allowing for autonomy.

In conclusion, Yemaya's stories of motherhood and caregiving in Yoruba mythology highlight her profound nurturing qualities and the complex dynamics of her relationships with the orishas. Her successes in raising powerful and positive figures like Shango and the Ibeji are testaments to her exceptional caregiving abilities. However, her challenges and occasional failures also offer valuable insights into the complexities of caregiving, emphasizing the importance of balance in nurturing relationships.

EXERCISES & RITUALS

Connecting with Yemaya and the Caregiver archetype can be enriched by incorporating elements of the ocean, reflecting her dominion over the seas and her nurturing nature. These exercises use the physical presence of the ocean or oceanic symbols to deepen the alignment with Yemaya and foster self-love, compassion, and balanced caregiving.

THE CAREGIVER

Beach Meditation and Offering

Supplies Needed:
- A small offering (such as flowers or fruits)
- Comfortable clothing
- A journal and pen

Guidelines:
1. Preparation: Choose a quiet beach where you can sit undisturbed. Dress comfortably and bring a small offering for Yemaya.
2. Arrival: As you arrive at the beach, take a moment to appreciate the ocean's vastness and beauty. Walk along the shoreline, feeling the sand under your feet and the water's touch.
3. Meditation: Find a comfortable spot to sit. Close your eyes, take deep breaths, and listen to the rhythmic sound of the waves. Visualize Yemaya emerging from the water, radiating nurturing energy.
4. Offering: Present your offering to the ocean as a gesture of gratitude to Yemaya. Place it gently in the water or on the shore, saying, "Yemaya, I offer this to you in gratitude for your guidance and nurturing energy."
5. Reflection: Spend a few moments reflecting on your intentions for caregiving and self-care. Write down any insights or commitments in your journal.
6. Affirmations: Stand at the water's edge and repeat affirmations such as, "I am nurtured and cared for," "I balance giving and receiving care," and "Yemaya's love flows through me."

Explanation:
This ritual strengthens the connection with Yemaya by directly engaging with her element, the ocean. It promotes a sense of peace, gratitude, and balance, helping to overcome self-neglect and embrace self-love.

Ocean Walk and Sea Shell Collection

<u>Supplies Needed</u>:
- A small basket or bag
- Comfortable walking shoes
- A journal and pen

<u>Guidelines</u>:
1. Preparation: Plan a visit to a beach with a variety of sea shells. Wear comfortable walking shoes and bring a small basket or bag for collecting shells.
2. Walk: Begin your walk along the shoreline, focusing on the natural beauty around you. As you walk, collect sea shells that catch your eye, appreciating their unique shapes and colors.
3. Mindfulness: Practice mindfulness during your walk by paying attention to the sensations of walking, the sound of the waves, and the feel of the shells in your hand. Use this time to clear your mind and focus on the present moment.
4. Reflection: After your walk, find a quiet spot to sit and reflect on your experience. Write down any thoughts or feelings in your journal, focusing on how the walk and the act of collecting shells made you feel.
5. Creating a Shell Altar: At home, create a small altar using the collected shells. Arrange them in a pleasing pattern and place a small blue or white candle in the center. This altar can serve as a daily reminder of Yemaya's presence and your connection to her nurturing energy.

<u>Explanation</u>:
This exercise combines physical activity with mindfulness and creativity, enhancing the connection to Yemaya through natural elements. It promotes a deeper sense of care for oneself and a balanced approach to caregiving.

Sea Shell Self-Care Ritual

<u>Supplies Needed</u>:
- A collection of sea shells
- A bowl of water
- Sea salt
- Essential oils (lavender or chamomile)
- A comfortable place to sit

<u>Guidelines</u>:
1. Preparation: Gather a collection of sea shells and arrange them around a bowl of water. Add sea salt and a few drops of essential oils to the water.
2. Meditation: Sit comfortably and close your eyes. Hold a sea shell in your hand, feeling its texture and weight. Visualize the ocean and Yemaya's nurturing presence.
3. Water Ritual: Dip the sea shell into the bowl of water and gently anoint your forehead, heart, and hands, saying, "Yemaya, bless me with your nurturing and loving energy. Help me to care for myself as I care for others."
4. Affirmations: Repeat affirmations such as, "I am worthy of love and care," "I nurture myself with compassion," and "I balance giving and receiving care."
5. Reflection: Spend a few moments reflecting on how you can incorporate more self-care into your daily routine. Write down any insights or commitments in your journal.

<u>Explanation</u>:
This ritual uses sea shells and water to connect with Yemaya's energy, promoting self-love and balanced caregiving. It helps individuals overcome self-neglect and embrace a nurturing attitude toward themselves.

Ocean Visualization and Creative Expression

<u>Supplies Needed</u>:
- A comfortable place to sit
- Blue and white colored pencils or paints
- Paper or canvas

<u>Guidelines</u>:
1. Preparation: Find a quiet and comfortable place to sit. Close your eyes and take several deep breaths to center yourself.
2. Visualization: Visualize yourself sitting by the ocean, feeling the gentle breeze and hearing the rhythmic waves. Imagine Yemaya emerging from the ocean, her presence radiating love and nurturing energy.
3. Creative Expression: Open your eyes and use the blue and white colored pencils or paints to create an image that represents Yemaya or your experience by the ocean. Let your creativity flow without judgment.
4. Affirmations: As you create, repeat affirmations such as, "I am a vessel of compassion and care," "I balance my needs with the needs of others," and "Yemaya's love flows through me."
5. Reflection: Spend a few moments reflecting on the experience and how it felt to express your connection to Yemaya creatively. Write down any thoughts or feelings in your journal.

<u>Explanation</u>:
This exercise combines visualization and creative expression to deepen the connection with Yemaya. It encourages self-reflection and creative release, helping individuals integrate Yemaya's nurturing energy into their lives.

The therapeutic potential of engaging with Yemaya lies in her ability to help individuals connect with their own nurturing and protective qualities. By invoking Yemaya through rituals and ceremonies, individuals can access her compassionate energy, fostering a sense of security and emotional healing. Engaging with Yemaya's energy can also help individuals develop a deeper sense of empathy and understanding, allowing them to connect with others on a profound emotional level.

Moreover, Yemaya's association with the ocean and water symbolizes purification and renewal. Engaging with Yemaya through rituals involving water, such as cleansing baths or offerings to the ocean, can help individuals release negative emotions and cleanse their spirit. This process of purification and renewal aligns with the path to individuation, allowing individuals to integrate the positive aspects of the Caregiver archetype while releasing the shadow aspects.

REFLECTIONS

The narrative of Yemaya, rich with symbols of nurturing, protection, and maternal affection, beautifully encapsulates the essence of the Caregiver archetype within Yoruba spirituality and beyond. Her tales, flowing like the waters she governs, remind us of the profound influence that caregiving can have on both individual lives and the broader community.

As the orisha of the oceans and motherhood, Yemaya's story teaches us about the depth of the Caregiver's capacity for love and sacrifice. Her protective nature, which ensures the safety and well-being of her children and all those who call upon her, mirrors the responsibilities held by all who adopt the Caregiver role. Through her, we see how nurturing can foster growth and resilience, and how the acts of caring reach far beyond immediate needs, supporting the emotional and spiritual growth of others.

Yemaya's presence in the pantheon also highlights the balance required in caregiving. She exemplifies the strength it takes to hold others up while also emphasizing the necessity of replenishing one's own spirit—a challenge familiar to anyone who cares deeply for others. Her ability to rule over the vast, nurturing yet sometimes tumultuous ocean serves as a metaphor for the Caregiver's journey: one must manage the immense task of caring without being overwhelmed by its demands.

Through Yemaya, we are invited to recognize and celebrate the essential role of Caregivers in our societies. Her stories urge those who identify with this archetype to embrace their nurturing instincts while also caring for themselves. Her influence teaches us that true caregiving does not deplete one's own resources but rather is a wellspring of mutual growth and enrichment.

Thus, as we draw inspiration from Yemaya, let us strive to embody the Caregiver in its most balanced and sustainable form. Let us be like the ocean she rules—deep and nurturing, strong and supportive, ever-present and life-sustaining. Let the legacy of Yemaya guide us in our caregiving endeavors, ensuring that we nurture not just those we love but also the communities and environments that sustain us all.

Chapter 7

The Explorer

The Explorer archetype, deeply rooted in Jungian psychology, symbolizes the universal quest for discovery, characterized by curiosity, independence, and the courage to venture into the unknown. This archetype is driven by an innate desire to break conventional boundaries and to discover new realms of experience and understanding. It embodies the human spirit's search for meaning beyond the familiar and comfortable, exploring new ideas, places, and spiritual insights.

In Jungian terms, the Explorer is part of the collective unconscious, representing a psychic counterpart of the instinct to seek and conquer. This archetype helps individuals negotiate the unknown terrains of life and facilitates personal growth and expansion beyond one's immediate environment. The Explorer is both a literal and metaphorical traveler, navigating physical distances and the internal landscapes of the mind and spirit.

Strengths and Weaknesses
The primary strength of the Explorer lies in their resilience and adaptability, which foster innovative thinking and creative problem-solving. However, these same strengths can manifest as weaknesses when the thirst for adventure overrides the need for stability, leading to feelings of aimlessness and dissatisfaction. Explorers may struggle with commitment, often in pursuit of new challenges, and may neglect deeper, meaningful connections or personal responsibilities.

Cultural Examples
The archetype is exemplified by figures such as Odysseus from Homer's *Odyssey*, who embodies the physical and psychological journey inherent to the Explorer. Similarly, characters like Indiana Jones and real-life figures like Marco Polo highlight the archetype's influence across cultures and epochs, illustrating its timeless appeal and relevance.

The Explorer archetype is more relevant than ever in a world that increasingly values personal freedom, innovation, and the pursuit of new experiences. In modern society, the Explorer is often associated with those who push the boundaries of knowledge and technology, such as scientists, entrepreneurs, and adventurers. Figures like Elon Musk, who is known for his ambitious goals of space exploration and technological advancement, embody the Explorer's drive to venture into the unknown and chart new territories.

In popular culture, the Explorer archetype is represented by characters who seek out new experiences and challenge the status quo. The film *Into the Wild*, based on the true story of Christopher McCandless, tells the tale of a young man who abandons conventional life in pursuit of a deeper connection with nature and self-discovery. The Explorer's journey is often one of personal growth and transformation, as individuals seek to find meaning and purpose in a world that is constantly changing.

Historical or Contemporary Figures
Amelia Earhart (1897–1937)
Amelia Earhart, the pioneering aviator, is a quintessential example of the Explorer archetype. Earhart's determination to push the boundaries of what was possible in aviation led her to become the first woman to fly solo across the Atlantic Ocean. Her adventurous spirit and courage continue to inspire those who seek to explore new horizons and challenge societal norms.

Marco Polo (1254–1324)
Marco Polo, the Venetian merchant and explorer, is another classic example of the Explorer archetype. Polo's travels to Asia and his detailed accounts of his experiences opened up new worlds to the people of Europe. His journey epitomizes the Explorer's quest for discovery, knowledge, and understanding of the unknown.

In Psychology
The Explorer archetype also has a strong presence in the realm of modern psychology, where it is associated with the desire for self-discovery and personal growth. Exploratory practices, such as travel therapy or wilderness retreats, encourage individuals to step outside their comfort zones and explore new aspects of themselves and the world around them. The rise of digital nomadism, where individuals work remotely while traveling the world, is another manifestation of the Explorer archetype in contemporary life. This archetype inspires individuals to seek out new experiences, embrace uncertainty, and continually evolve.

Shadow Side
The shadow aspect of the Explorer archetype emerges when the desire for adventure and discovery transforms into escapism. This can manifest as an avoidance of deeper personal or societal responsibilities, where the pursuit of freedom becomes an excuse to evade commitments and meaningful connections. The Explorer may find themselves in a perpetual state of restlessness, unable to settle or find contentment, constantly seeking new

experiences without fully integrating the lessons learned from each journey. This shadow side can lead to a sense of disorientation or even alienation, as the Explorer becomes disconnected from the very society and community that provide a grounding influence.

Path to Individuation
The path to individuation for the Explorer involves striking a balance between the innate desire for freedom and the need for responsibility. This process requires the Explorer to integrate their diverse experiences into a cohesive identity that honors both their adventurous spirit and their obligations to themselves and others. It is through this balance that the Explorer can transform potentially aimless wandering into a purposeful journey of self-discovery. By acknowledging the importance of stability and commitment, the Explorer can contribute meaningfully to the broader community while continuing their quest for new horizons. This integration allows the Explorer to become a well-rounded individual who not only seeks out new experiences but also understands the value of reflecting on those experiences and using them to grow and support others.

OCHOSI AS THE EXPLORER

Ochosi, the Yoruba orisha of hunting and the wilderness, epitomizes the Explorer archetype through his mastery of the hunt and his deep connection with the natural world. Known for his sharp eyesight and impeccable aim, Ochosi is a symbol of focused pursuit, embodying the Explorer's drive to seek out and uncover hidden truths.

Connection to the Explorer Archetype
Ochosi's role as a hunter requires a profound understanding of his environment, mirroring the Explorer's navigation through uncharted territories. His life in the wilderness demands independence, strategic thinking, and an intimate knowledge of his surroundings, qualities that are quintessential to the Explorer.

THE EXPLORER

Strengths and Weaknesses
Ochosi's strengths include his precision and strategic expertise, which enable him to excel in hunting and tracking. These skills translate into spiritual and moral dimensions, guiding his followers in their quests for justice and truth. However, Ochosi's intense focus can also be a weakness, leading to isolation and a potential neglect of communal duties and relationships. His solitary nature may cause him to drift away from societal connections, reflecting the Explorer's shadow of disconnection and loneliness.

Shadow Side and Path to Individuation
The shadow side of Ochosi manifests as a tendency towards solitude and moral ambiguity, where his skills as a hunter could lead to a disconnection from the community. His path to individuation involves balancing his solitary pursuits with his responsibilities to his community. By integrating his exploratory drives with a commitment to societal values, Ochosi can achieve a harmonious existence, utilizing his skills for the greater good and fostering a deeper connection with both the spiritual and communal realms.

OCHOSI STORIES

Ochosi features prominently in several significant myths that illustrate his complex character and his interactions with other orishas. Two of the most poignant tales involve his deep friendship with Ogun and the tragic incident of inadvertently killing his mother. These stories not only reflect his attributes as the Explorer but also his moral and ethical challenges.

Ochosi and Ogun: The Bond of Brotherhood
One of the most celebrated stories in Yoruba mythology involves the partnership between Ochosi and Ogun. Ogun, the orisha of iron and war, is often depicted as a fierce warrior with a robust and sometimes uncontrollable character. His strength and skill in crafting and warfare make him a powerful figure within the pantheon. Ochosi, known for his precision

and strategic thinking, complements Ogun's might with his own finesse and tactical acumen.

The tale begins when Ochosi and Ogun find themselves needing to combine their skills to achieve a common goal. In the dense forest where hunting and survival are paramount, Ochosi's sharp eyesight and expert archery were ideally paired with Ogun's strength and mastery over metal. Together, they embarked on a hunt that required both Ochosi's ability to track and target and Ogun's power to clear the path and craft weapons.

Their collaboration proved to be supremely effective, leading them to share many successful exploits. Through these shared experiences, a deep bond of friendship and respect was forged between them, highlighting themes of unity and the strength found in complementary partnerships. This alliance also symbolizes the integration of different aspects of the self, as represented by Ochosi's strategic mind and Ogun's strength, illustrating a holistic approach to challenges.

Cultural Significance
This story is often interpreted as a metaphor for the necessity of balancing different forces in life—thought and action, strategy and strength. It underscores the value of collaboration and the importance of relationships in achieving one's goals. In religious ceremonies, Ochosi and Ogun are frequently invoked together, symbolizing their inseparable connection and the believers' desire for balanced assistance in their endeavors.

The Tragic Tale of Ochosi's Misjudgment
In a poignant narrative within Yoruba mythology, Ochosi faces a grave moral and personal crisis, which underscores his role as a seeker of justice and the potential for tragic error even in well-intentioned acts.

Ochosi, known for his unmatched skills as a hunter, often dedicated his hunt to Olofin, the supreme ruler, by presenting him with the best of his captures.

However, a mysterious figure repeatedly stole the birds Ochosi hunted before he could present them to Olofin. Driven to resolve this affront and restore his offerings to Olofin, Ochosi used his skills to track down the thief.

Lying in wait, determined to catch the perpetrator, Ochosi prepared his bow and arrow. When he saw movement and a figure approaching his trap, without hesitation, he released his arrow. To his horror, he discovered that he had not shot a common thief, but his own mother, who had been taking the birds to feed her family, unaware of her son's intentions to offer them to Olofin. The realization of his tragic mistake devastated Ochosi, casting a long shadow of grief and remorse over him.

Cultural and Psychological Interpretations
This story serves as a poignant reminder of the shadow side of the Explorer archetype—the potential for overzealous actions to lead to unforeseen consequences. In Jungian terms, this tale can be seen as a dramatic representation of the conflicts and psychic tensions experienced during the individuation process, where unintended consequences force a reevaluation of one's actions and motivations. The tragedy of killing his mother brings Ochosi to a deeper understanding of his powers and responsibilities, pushing him toward a more tempered and cautious approach to justice.

Ochosi's tragic mistake is a pivotal story that resonates deeply within the Yoruba spiritual framework and beyond. It illustrates the complex interplay between justice and error, intention and outcome, reminding followers of the orisha to seek balance and understanding in their actions. This story enriches the narrative of Ochosi as an Explorer, deeply committed to his duties yet vulnerable to the very human predicament of error, making his journey an enduring lesson in humility and the pursuit of ethical integrity.

The tales of Ochosi's deep friendship with Ogun and the tragic killing of his mother offer rich insights into his character as an orisha. They reflect the themes of partnership, justice, tragedy, and personal growth, which are central to understanding his role within the Yoruba pantheon and his appeal as a figure of veneration in the African diaspora religions. These stories underscore the complexity of Ochosi's character and his enduring relevance as a symbol of the quest for balance between action and foresight.

EXERCISES & RITUALS

Aligning with Ochosi and the Explorer archetype involves embracing a spirit of adventure and justice while mitigating the risks of rashness and isolation. Here are some exercises and rituals designed to cultivate balance, thoughtful decision-making, and collaborative success.

Collaborative Mapping Exercise

Supplies Needed:
- Large paper or whiteboard
- Markers or colored pens
- Sticky notes

Guidelines:
1. Preparation: Gather a small group of friends or colleagues. Provide each person with markers and sticky notes.
2. Activity: On the large paper or whiteboard, draw a map outline that represents a goal or project.
3. Collaboration: Invite participants to use sticky notes to add ideas, obstacles, and resources they believe are relevant to achieving the goal. Encourage discussion and negotiation about where each element should be placed on the map.
4. Strategy Development: As a group, decide on pathways through the obstacles to the goal, illustrating how collaborative efforts can lead to successful outcomes.

5. Reflection: Discuss what each participant has learned about cooperation and how the exercise might influence their approach to group projects or goals in the future.

Explanation:
This exercise promotes understanding and appreciation for collaborative processes, a vital skill for Explorers who often venture solo but need to integrate their journeys with larger community or team objectives.

Ritual of Balance

Supplies Needed:
- Two small bowls
- Water
- A handful of soil
- Candle

Guidelines:
1. Setup: Place the bowls on a flat surface. Fill one bowl with water and the other with soil. Light a candle between them.
2. Ritual Action: Reflect on the symbolism of each element—water as flexibility and adaptability, soil as stability and grounding.
3. Balancing Act: Slowly pour water into the bowl with soil, mixing them until you achieve a balanced consistency, neither too muddy nor too dry.
4. Meditation and Prayer: As you mix, meditate on achieving balance in your own life, particularly in how you make decisions. Pray to Ochosi for the wisdom to know when to move quickly and when to be steady and grounded.
5. Closing: Extinguish the candle as a sign of completing the ritual. Commit to applying the balance you've cultivated in this ritual to your daily actions.

Explanation:
This ritual helps the practitioner internalize the concept of balance between action and reflection, encouraging a harmonious approach to the Explorer's typical impulsivity and isolation. It serves as a physical metaphor for the internal work necessary to moderate the Explorer's extremes.

Arrow Crafting Workshop

Supplies Needed:
- Wooden dowels or sticks
- Feathers
- String
- Beads and other decorative items
- Tools for carving and crafting (safely supervised)

Guidelines:
1. Preparation: Gather all materials and set up a crafting station. If possible, conduct this workshop in a natural setting or a well-ventilated area.
2. Crafting Session: Start the session with a brief introduction to Ochosi, emphasizing his precision and skill as an archer. Explain how each part of the arrow symbolizes aspects of decision-making (shaft for direction, feathers for balance, and point for precision).
3. Interactive Crafting: As participants craft their arrows, encourage them to reflect on a specific decision or goal they are currently considering. Instruct them to imbue their arrow with intentions related to clarity, focus, and balance.
4. Sharing Circle: Once the arrows are crafted, gather in a circle and invite participants to share what their arrow represents and how this craft helps them visualize achieving their goals.
5. Conclusion: Emphasize the importance of precision and thoughtfulness in actions and decisions, mirroring the careful crafting of an arrow.

Explanation:
This workshop not only fosters creativity but also serves as a metaphorical exercise in focusing and directing one's energy and intentions, essential for maintaining the balanced path of the Explorer.

Compass Navigation Challenge

Supplies Needed:
- Compasses
- Maps of a local park or safe wilderness area
- List of waypoints or landmarks

Guidelines:
1. Preparation: Organize a small group outing to a local park or wilderness area. Provide each participant with a map and a compass.
2. Challenge Instructions: Each participant or team is given a series of waypoints or landmarks they must find using only their map and compass.
3. Teamwork Emphasis: Encourage participants to work in teams, fostering discussion and cooperation to find the best route to each landmark.
4. Reflection and Discussion: After completing the challenge, discuss as a group what was learned about navigating and working together. Highlight the importance of each team member's input and how multiple perspectives lead to better decision-making.
5. Debrief: Conclude with insights on how this exercise applies to daily life challenges, emphasizing the need for strategic planning and cooperative problem-solving.

Explanation:
This activity directly engages with Ochosi's skills in navigation and strategy, while also teaching valuable lessons in teamwork and the practical application of Explorer traits in collective settings.

These exercises and rituals enrich the experience of aligning with Ochosi and the Explorer archetype, offering diverse ways to integrate these energies into practical and reflective activities that foster personal growth and community connection.

REFLECTIONS

Ochosi's story, as it unfolds within the rich tapestry of Yoruba mythology, captures the essence of the Explorer archetype with profound depth and clarity. His narrative, woven with themes of adventure, justice, and the quest for knowledge, serves as a powerful reflection on the nature of exploration—both of the world around us and the landscapes within us.

The tales of Ochosi, from his expert navigation of the wilderness to his strategic prowess in hunting, underscore the attributes that define the Explorer: curiosity, courage, and a relentless drive to push beyond known boundaries. These stories not only highlight his physical journeys but also illuminate his spiritual and moral quests, reflecting the Explorer's role in transcending mere physical travel to embrace a journey toward greater understanding and enlightenment.

Ochosi's integration into the pantheon of orishas as the quintessential hunter and guide offers valuable insights into how exploration can be a conduit for greater societal and personal development. His ability to use his keen sight for justice positions him as a figure who not only explores but also protects and serves, reinforcing the idea that the true Explorer does not venture forth for selfish reasons but to discover ways to contribute positively to the world.

THE EXPLORER

Moreover, Ochosi's narrative invites those who resonate with the Explorer archetype to consider the broader implications of their quests. It challenges individuals to ponder how their explorations can bring not only personal growth but also benefit others—whether by paving new paths, as Ochosi did for the orishas, or by using their discoveries to advocate for justice and truth. His story is a reminder that the journeys we undertake can have profound impacts, influencing not just our own lives but also the fabric of our communities.

Therefore, as we draw inspiration from Ochosi's example, let us strive to be Explorers in the fullest sense: those who seek not only to chart unknown territories but to understand their deeper meanings, those who use their discoveries to illuminate and protect, and those who, above all, journey with a sense of responsibility and purpose. Ochosi's legacy teaches us that exploration is as much about the paths we clear for others as it is about the journeys we embark upon ourselves.

Chapter 8

The Rebel

The Rebel archetype, deeply embedded in the collective unconscious, represents a challenge to authority and a profound disruption of the status quo. Those who embody this archetype are often seen as agents of change, motivated by a vision to overturn what they perceive as oppressive or outdated structures. They are characterized by an unwavering commitment to revolution and a deep-seated disdain for conventional norms.

Characteristics and Traits
The Rebel is driven by a desire for autonomy and self-determination. They thrive in environments that allow for innovation and often emerge in times of social upheaval where traditional systems are no longer viable. The Rebel's journey is one of transformation, marked by a relentless pursuit of a new order that aligns with their ideals of justice and equality. Their ability to inspire and mobilize others is one of their greatest strengths, making them charismatic leaders in movements for social change.

However, the path of the Rebel is fraught with challenges. Their aversion to authority and structure can manifest as a stubborn resistance to anything that resembles control, which can hinder their ability to effect sustainable change. Moreover, their intense focus on dismantling existing systems can sometimes overshadow the equally important task of building new ones. This can leave them vulnerable to the temptations of power once the revolution they championed comes to fruition, potentially becoming the very forces they originally opposed.

Cultural Examples
Historically, Rebels have appeared in various forms across cultures and stories, often becoming heroic figures in their societies. In literature, characters like Robin Hood, who steals from the rich to give to the poor, challenge unjust economic systems and embody the Rebel's fight for social justice. In film, characters such as Max Rockatansky from the *Mad Max* films or The Bride from Quentin Tarantino's *Kill Bill* series represent the Rebel's fight against oppressive forces to reclaim personal agency and integrity.

The Rebel archetype is a powerful force in contemporary society, particularly in movements that challenge established norms and fight for social change. This archetype is embodied by activists, revolutionaries, and nonconformists who refuse to accept the status quo and instead seek to transform society. Figures like Rosa Parks, whose refusal to give up her seat on a segregated bus sparked the Civil Rights Movement, exemplify the Rebel's capacity to inspire change through defiance.

In popular culture, the Rebel archetype is often portrayed by characters who challenge authority and fight for justice. The *Star Wars* franchise, with its portrayal of the Rebel Alliance fighting against the oppressive Galactic Empire, captures the essence of the Rebel archetype's struggle against tyranny. Similarly, dystopian novels like *The Hunger Games* depict protagonists who rise up against corrupt systems, embodying the Rebel's desire for freedom and justice.

Historical or Contemporary Figures
Rosa Parks (1913–2005)
Rosa Parks, often referred to as "the mother of the civil rights movement," exemplifies the Rebel archetype through her courageous defiance of racial segregation laws in the United States. On December 1, 1955, Parks refused to give up her seat to a white passenger on a segregated bus in Montgomery, Alabama. Her act of civil disobedience sparked the Montgomery Bus Boycott and became a pivotal moment in the fight for civil rights. Parks' rebellion against unjust laws and her role in challenging systemic oppression make her a powerful symbol of the Rebel archetype, demonstrating how one individual's courage can ignite widespread social change.

Malcolm X (1925–1965)
Malcolm X, born Malcolm Little, was an African American Muslim minister and human rights activist who became one of the most influential figures in the fight for civil rights during the 20th century. Known for his outspoken and uncompromising stance on racial justice, Malcolm X challenged the prevailing attitudes of racial segregation and inequality in the United States. His advocacy for Black empowerment, self-defense, and the rejection of integration as the only path to equality made him a controversial and revolutionary figure.

Malcolm X's transformation from a street hustler to a leading voice for African American rights embodies the Rebel's journey of defiance against established norms and the pursuit of radical change. His life and speeches continue to inspire those who seek to challenge and reform societal injustices, making him a powerful example of the Rebel archetype.

In Psychology
The Rebel archetype also plays a significant role in modern psychology, where it is associated with the process of individuation and self-actualization. This archetype encourages individuals to break free from societal expectations and explore their true selves. In therapeutic settings, the Rebel

archetype may be invoked to help clients challenge limiting beliefs and behaviors, empowering them to take control of their lives and make meaningful changes. The Rebel's influence is evident in contemporary movements for social justice, environmental activism, and personal empowerment, where individuals and groups work to create a more equitable and sustainable world.

Shadow Side and Path to Individuation
The shadow side of the Rebel emerges when their methods become as oppressive as the systems they aim to overthrow. This typically occurs when the desire for change turns into an obsession, leading to justification of all means to achieve their ends, including violence and coercion. For true individuation, the Rebel must integrate their transformative desires with a balanced approach that values not just the tearing down of old ways but the responsible creation of new ones. They must learn to negotiate rather than dominate, seeking solutions that harmonize their need for independence with the community's need for order and stability.

OGUN AS THE REBEL

Ogun, the Yoruba orisha of iron, war, and pathways, is a quintessential example of the Rebel archetype. As a deity who both creates and destroys, Ogun's dual nature makes him a complex figure in Yoruba cosmology and religion. His role as a path-clearer and a warrior symbolizes the Rebel's function as both a liberator and a challenger of the status quo.

Connection to the Rebel Archetype
Ogun's mythology is filled with stories of his role in clearing forests and battling unseen enemies, paving the way for civilization and order. Yet, he is also known for his wild, untamed nature, which speaks to the Rebel's inner conflict between creating change and controlling the chaos that change can bring. Ogun's tools—the knife and the anvil—are symbols of his ability to shape and reshape society, reflecting the Rebel's transformative power.

THE REBEL

His spiritual and cultural significance extends beyond the mythological to the everyday lives of those who worship him. Ogun is revered as the patron saint of blacksmiths, warriors, and all who work with metal. His festivals and rituals, involving the spilling of palm wine, the sacrifice of dogs, and loud, rhythmic drumming, are not merely celebrations but reenactments of his revolutionary spirit.

Strengths and Weaknesses
Ogun's strengths lie in his determination and his capacity to fight for justice. He is a protector of the oppressed, a quality that endears him to his followers. However, his aggressive nature can lead to destructiveness if not properly channeled. His impulsive actions have sometimes resulted in tragic consequences, as seen in myths where his fury leads to unintended harm to those he loves or to himself.

Path to Individuation
For Ogun, achieving individuation requires finding a balance between his destructive capabilities and his creative potential. He must learn to temper his aggression with foresight and his rebellious spirit with wisdom. By focusing on his role as a creator and not just a destroyer, Ogun can fulfill the true potential of the Rebel archetype, leading not just to revolution but to lasting reform and renewal.

OGUN STORIES

Ogun, a powerful and complex figure, embodies the duality of creation and destruction, innovation and chaos. His journey to becoming the orisha of iron is intertwined with tales of his successes, failures, and moments of profound transformation, revealing the depth and breadth of his character.

The Genesis of Ogun as the Orisha of Iron

The story of how Ogun became associated with iron is foundational to understanding his role in Yoruba cosmology. Iron, in Yoruba culture, is not merely a metal; it is the embodiment of potential and power, capable of creating tools for building societies or weapons for tearing them down. According to the myth, Ogun was the first orisha to descend to Earth, using a metal anvil and his knowledge to forge paths, tools, and weapons. He introduced the use of iron to humanity, teaching them how to harness its power for agriculture, warfare, and crafts. This gift of iron profoundly changed human society, facilitating agricultural development, political power, and artistic expression.

Successes and Transformations

Ogun's introduction of iron tools and weapons marks one of his greatest successes, as it played a crucial role in the advancement of human civilizations. With his tools, communities could till the land more efficiently, hunters could provide more for their families, and warriors could defend their territories. Ogun's ability to manipulate iron also symbolizes the transformation of raw materials into useful objects, mirroring his role as a transformer not just of physical substances but of cultural and social landscapes.

However, Ogun's power was not without its perils. His mastery of iron also brought about the tools of war and destruction, inadvertently teaching humanity not only to build but also to destroy. This duality is a constant theme in Ogun's myths, reflecting the dual nature of technology and power.

The Fall from Grace: The Defilement of His Mother

One of Ogun's most tragic tales involves his fall from grace through the accidental defilement of his mother. In a fit of rage induced by intoxication, Ogun, unaware of his actions, committed this grave act. This story starkly portrays the destructive potential of Ogun's power when not controlled, leading to catastrophic consequences that deeply affected him and his divine family.

The guilt and horror of his actions led Ogun into a profound depression, causing him to retreat into the wilderness, withdrawing from the world he had helped to create. This self-imposed exile reflects his deep sense of responsibility and the overwhelming burden of his guilt.

Redemption: The Role of Oshun
Ogun's story does not end in despair, thanks to Oshun, the orisha of water, fertility, and love. Seeing the suffering that Ogun's absence was causing to the world—tools broke, and no one could repair them, warriors were defenseless, and chaos reigned—Oshun decided to intervene. She used her charm and sweetness, symbolized by her honey, to lure Ogun out of his isolation. By offering honey, she not only physically drew him out but also metaphorically healed his bitterness with her sweetness and love.

Oshun's successful retrieval of Ogun from the wilderness signifies the healing power of love and compassion, elements that temper the harshness of iron and war. This act restored balance, allowing Ogun to return with a renewed sense of purpose, emphasizing the necessity of balancing masculine and feminine energies, strength and gentleness, power and mercy.

Ogun's narrative is a compelling exploration of the complexities of power, responsibility, and redemption. His journey through success, failure, and eventual reconciliation encapsulates the challenges faced by those who wield great power and the continuous need for balance and reflection. His stories not only teach about the responsibilities that come with power but also about the possibility of redemption and the powerful role of compassion in the process of healing and restoration.

EXERCISES & RITUALS

Aligning with Ogun and the Rebel archetype involves channeling the energies of change and resistance into constructive and positive actions. The following exercises and rituals are designed to help harness these powerful energies while mitigating their potential for destructiveness, focusing on transformation, empowerment, and responsible action.

Iron Meditation and Visualization

Supplies Needed:
- A small iron object, such as a nail or a small tool
- A quiet, comfortable place for meditation

Guidelines:
1. Setup: Sit in a quiet space where you won't be disturbed. Hold the iron object in your hands to serve as a focal point for your meditation.
2. Meditation: Close your eyes and take deep, slow breaths. Focus on the weight and texture of the iron in your hands, feeling its solidity and strength.
3. Visualization: Visualize the iron glowing with a warm light, representing Ogun's power. Imagine this light spreading from the object into your body, symbolizing the absorption of Ogun's strength and resilience.
4. Intention Setting: Reflect on areas of your life where you need to implement change or stand up for your beliefs. Visualize yourself using Ogun's strength to approach these situations with courage but also with wisdom and calm.
5. Conclude: End your meditation by envisioning the warm light being channeled into a specific action or decision that leads to a positive change in your life. Gently open your eyes and make a commitment to carry this strength and intention into your daily interactions.

Explanation:
This meditation helps to internalize Ogun's attributes of strength and transformation, while the focus on controlled breathing and visualization promotes calmness, helping to mitigate impulsiveness and aggression.

Path-Clearing Ritual

Supplies Needed:
- A machete or a representation of one (for safety)
- Several small obstacles or blocks (stones or small boxes)
- An open space where a path can be laid out

Guidelines:
1. Preparation: Arrange the obstacles along a path in the open space, symbolizing the barriers you face in life.
2. Ritual Action: Begin at one end of the path with the machete in hand. As you walk the path, gently move each obstacle aside with the machete, clearing the way as you go.
3. Affirmations: As you move each obstacle, recite affirmations such as, "I remove this barrier with thought and precision," reinforcing the idea of using power responsibly.
4. Reflection: Once the path is clear, reflect on the act of removing obstacles. Consider how the physical action can be a metaphor for addressing challenges in your life, emphasizing thoughtful action over rash behavior.
5. Closing: Store the machete away as a symbolic gesture of putting away your power until it is needed again, underlining the importance of control and discretion.

Explanation:
This ritual physically enacts the process of overcoming challenges, emphasizing the use of strength and power in a controlled and deliberate

manner, which is crucial for handling the Rebel's potential for destructiveness.

Community Service Action

Supplies Needed:
- Tools or materials specific to the chosen service activity
- A community or group setting

Guidelines:
1. Planning: Choose a community service activity that resonates with your values and where you feel you can make a difference, such as restoring a local park, helping at a community kitchen, or organizing a recycling drive.
2. Engagement: Involve yourself fully in the activity, using your skills and energy to contribute positively. Work alongside others to foster a sense of teamwork and shared purpose.
3. Reflection: After the activity, spend some time reflecting on how your efforts have helped the community. Consider how the act of service can be a powerful outlet for the Rebel's drive for change, channeling energy into productive and constructive actions.
4. Commitment: Make a commitment to regular involvement in community service, recognizing this as a way to continuously channel the Rebel energy positively and maintain alignment with Ogun's transformative spirit.

Explanation:
Engaging in community service allows the Rebel within to manifest through positive actions that benefit others, providing a productive outlet for the energies of change and resistance. This helps mitigate the shadow aspects of aggression and destructiveness by replacing them with community upliftment and cooperative achievements.

Forge Creation Meditation

Supplies Needed:
- A quiet space with minimal distractions
- Ambient sounds of a forge or workshop (available as recordings online)
- A comfortable place to sit or lie down

Guidelines:
1. Setup: Prepare your space by setting up the audio equipment to play the sounds of a forge—hammering, the roar of the fire, and the clinking of metal.
2. Meditation: Sit or lie down comfortably, close your eyes, and start the ambient forge sounds. Begin focusing on your breathing, slowly inhaling and exhaling to the rhythm of the forge.
3. Visualization: Visualize yourself in a forge, standing in front of an anvil. Imagine a raw piece of metal on the anvil that represents a personal challenge or a barrier you face.
4. Transformation: As you listen to the sounds of the forge, visualize yourself heating and hammering the metal into a new shape, transforming it into a useful tool. With each strike, see the metal taking shape, symbolizing your ability to reshape and adapt challenges into opportunities.
5. Reflection and Commitment: Reflect on the process of transformation and how you can apply this in real life. Commit to using this newly forged tool (metaphorically) to tackle challenges in your life, reminding yourself that you have the power to transform obstacles into assets.

Explanation:
This meditation links the physical process of forging with mental and emotional transformation. It helps in internalizing the Rebel's capacity to

convert adversities into advantages, reinforcing positive outcomes from aggressive energies.

REFLECTIONS

The tales of Ogun, from his pioneering introduction of iron to his profound moments of personal crisis, encapsulate the essence of the Rebel archetype within Yoruba mythology. His story is a vivid reminder of the transformative power of rebellion, the potential for both creation and destruction, and the necessity for moral introspection in wielding such power. Ogun's journey through innovation, error, withdrawal, and redemption offers profound lessons on the complexities of leadership and the responsibilities that come with it.

Ogun's narrative serves as a rich source of inspiration and caution for those who find resonance with the Rebel archetype. His successes highlight the potential for positive change and societal advancement when power is used wisely. His failures, particularly the tragic incident with his mother, illustrate the dangers of unchecked aggression and the deep consequences of our actions. Yet, his redemption through Oshun's intervention teaches that healing and reconciliation are possible, emphasizing the importance of compassion and empathy in overcoming personal and collective crises.

The archetype of the Rebel, as embodied by Ogun, challenges us to consider the balance between disruption and construction, between tearing down old structures and building new ones. It invites us to reflect on our own lives and the roles we play within our communities. Are we agents of constructive change, or does our rebellion lead to chaos? How do we respond to our own failures, and are we open to the healing powers of forgiveness and compassion?

Ogun's story, therefore, is not just about the past; it resonates in the present and offers guidance for the future. It encourages us to harness our rebellious energies not just with courage but with wisdom, to seek balance in our actions, and to remember that the road to transformation is often paved with challenges that require both our strength and our heart. As we navigate our paths, let us draw on the lessons from Ogun's life, striving to be rebels with a cause, rebels who not only fight against but also fight for—for justice, for progress, and for the betterment of humanity.

Chapter 9

The Lover

The Lover archetype, within the framework of Jungian psychology, represents the human capacity for profound connection, passion, and devotion. This archetype is the embodiment of the human desire to merge with others, to experience love in its fullest expression, and to engage deeply with the beauty of life. At its core, the Lover seeks out relationships and experiences that evoke intense emotional and sensual responses, driven by a need for intimacy and unity.

The Lover is characterized by their deep passion and zest for life. Individuals who embody this archetype are often seen as enthusiastic, empathetic, and deeply connected to their emotions. They have a natural ability to inspire others through their vibrancy and warmth, often becoming the heart and soul of their social circles. The Lover's commitment to their passions can manifest in romantic relationships, artistic pursuits, or any endeavor that ignites their spirit. This intense engagement with life makes the Lover a conduit for creativity and inspiration, fostering a sense of vitality in those around them.

However, the Lover's intense passion can also lead to potential weaknesses. When unbalanced, their desire for connection can become obsessive, leading to dependency and an inability to maintain boundaries. The Lover must learn to channel their passion in healthy ways, avoiding the pitfalls of infatuation and possessiveness. This journey towards balance involves cultivating a deeper understanding of oneself and learning to appreciate solitude as much as connection. The Lover's path is one of self-awareness and personal growth, requiring a nuanced approach to relationships that honors both individuality and togetherness.

Strengths and Weaknesses
The Lover's greatest strength lies in their capacity to forge meaningful connections and bring beauty and joy into the lives of those around them. Their ability to empathize and connect on a deep emotional level can foster profound relationships and inspire creative expression. The Lover sees beauty in the world where others might not, and this perspective allows them to appreciate and enhance the richness of life. They are often the ones who can lift the spirits of those around them, bringing color and vitality to their environments.

However, these strengths can become weaknesses if the Lover loses themselves in their passions. The intense desire for connection can lead to obsessive behaviors and a tendency to prioritize others' needs over their own. This can result in a loss of personal identity, as the Lover becomes consumed by their relationships and emotions. The challenge for the Lover is to maintain their sense of self while navigating the complexities of love and connection. This requires a conscious effort to establish healthy boundaries and to cultivate self-love, ensuring that their passion enhances rather than diminishes their sense of self.

Cultural Examples
The Lover archetype is prevalent in literature and film, often depicted as characters who pursue love and beauty with fervor and dedication. In

Shakespeare's *Romeo and Juliet*, the titular characters epitomize the Lover archetype, driven by an intense and tragic passion for one another. Their story is a testament to the transformative power of love and its potential to transcend societal boundaries, but it also serves as a cautionary tale about the dangers of unchecked passion. Similarly, in modern cinema, characters like Jack and Rose from *Titanic* exemplify the Lover's journey, where love becomes both a source of profound joy and a catalyst for personal transformation.

Beyond romantic narratives, the Lover archetype is also seen in figures who passionately pursue creative or spiritual paths. Artists like Vincent van Gogh and poets like Pablo Neruda exemplify the Lover's drive to capture beauty and emotion in their work. Their art is a manifestation of the Lover's quest for connection and meaning, reflecting the depth of their emotional experiences and their desire to share these with the world. These cultural examples illustrate the diverse ways in which the Lover archetype can manifest, highlighting both its transformative potential and its inherent challenges.

Historical or Contemporary Figures
Cleopatra (69 BCE–30 BCE)
Cleopatra, the last active ruler of the Ptolemaic Kingdom of Egypt, exemplifies the Lover archetype through her passionate relationships with Julius Caesar and Mark Antony. Cleopatra's life was marked by intense love, political intrigue, and her determination to maintain Egypt's independence. Her legacy as a powerful and enigmatic ruler who was deeply connected to her lovers continues to captivate the imagination.

Pablo Neruda (1904–1973)
Pablo Neruda, the Chilean poet, is another embodiment of the Lover archetype. Neruda's poetry is renowned for its intense emotion, passion, and celebration of love in all its forms. His work captures the essence of the

Lover archetype, with its focus on connection, beauty, and the transformative power of love.

In Psychology
The Lover archetype also finds expression in modern psychology, particularly in discussions about attachment, intimacy, and self-love. In therapeutic settings, the Lover archetype may be explored to help individuals understand their patterns of attachment and emotional connection, guiding them towards healthier and more fulfilling relationships. The emphasis on self-love and self-care in contemporary culture also reflects the Lover archetype's influence, encouraging individuals to cultivate a deep and compassionate relationship with themselves.

In the broader context of society, the Lover archetype is often invoked in discussions about the importance of empathy and compassion in building strong communities. Movements that promote inclusivity, diversity, and social connection resonate with the Lover's desire for unity and harmony. The rise of social media platforms that facilitate connection and intimacy, despite physical distances, also speaks to the Lover archetype's enduring relevance. In a world that is increasingly interconnected yet often fragmented, the Lover archetype reminds us of the power of love and connection to heal and unite.

Shadow Side
The shadow side of the Lover emerges when passion becomes obsession and the desire for connection leads to unhealthy attachments. This can manifest as jealousy, possessiveness, and a lack of personal boundaries, where the Lover's need for intimacy overrides their sense of self. In such cases, the Lover may become consumed by their emotions, losing sight of their individuality and becoming overly reliant on others for validation and fulfillment. This can lead to destructive patterns in relationships, as the Lover's intense emotions become a source of conflict rather than connection.

Navigating the shadow side of the Lover requires a conscious effort to balance passion with perspective. It involves recognizing the importance of personal boundaries and cultivating a strong sense of self-worth that is independent of external validation. The Lover must learn to appreciate the beauty of solitude and to find fulfillment in their own company, allowing their relationships to be a source of joy rather than a necessity. By embracing their individuality and nurturing their own passions, the Lover can transform their shadow into a source of strength and resilience.

Path to Individuation
For the Lover, the path to individuation involves integrating their passion with a sense of self-awareness and personal boundaries. It requires balancing their desire for connection with the need for independence, learning to love without losing themselves. This journey towards individuation is marked by a deepening understanding of oneself and a commitment to personal growth. The Lover learns to appreciate the value of solitude and to cultivate a rich inner life, allowing their relationships to enhance rather than define their identity.

By cultivating a deep love for themselves and their own life, the Lover can experience relationships as enriching rather than consuming, achieving a harmonious integration of their emotional and personal growth. This process of individuation is not about diminishing the Lover's passion but about channeling it in ways that are sustainable and fulfilling. By embracing their unique qualities and nurturing their own desires, the Lover can create a life that is both passionate and balanced, allowing their love to be a source of strength and inspiration.

OSHUN AS THE LOVER

Oshun, the Yoruba orisha of love, beauty, and fertility, embodies the Lover archetype in its most enchanting form. As a goddess associated with rivers,

Oshun is celebrated for her sensuality, charm, and nurturing qualities. Her presence in Yoruba mythology is one of profound beauty and irresistible allure, captivating all who encounter her. Oshun is often depicted as a radiant figure adorned with gold and jewels, symbolizing her connection to wealth and abundance. Her mythology is rich with tales of her passionate nature and her ability to foster love and harmony.

Connection to the Lover Archetype
Oshun's role as a mediator among the orishas further highlights her capacity to foster unity and connection. She is often called upon to resolve conflicts and to bring people together, using her charm and diplomacy to create harmony. Oshun's influence extends beyond romantic relationships, as she embodies the Lover's drive to connect with the world in meaningful ways. Her ability to inspire love and beauty wherever she goes is a testament to the transformative power of the Lover archetype, reminding us of the importance of connection and compassion in our lives.

Cultural Impact and Spiritual Significance
In Yoruba and diasporic traditions such as Santería and Candomblé, Oshun is revered as a powerful and benevolent deity who oversees matters of the heart and fertility. Her rituals often involve offerings of honey, oranges, and cinnamon, all symbolizing sweetness and allure. Followers of Oshun invoke her blessings in matters of love, fertility, and creativity, seeking her guidance in forming harmonious relationships and cultivating personal beauty. Her influence is felt in the everyday lives of her devotees, as she provides comfort and inspiration in times of need.

Oshun's cultural significance extends beyond her role as a deity, as she embodies the values of love, compassion, and empathy that are central to the human experience. Her presence in the lives of her followers is a reminder of the importance of nurturing relationships and fostering connections that enrich our lives. Oshun teaches us that true beauty lies in our ability to love and be loved, and that our relationships are a reflection of the love we cultivate within ourselves.

Strengths and Weaknesses
Oshun's strengths are evident in her ability to inspire love and beauty wherever she goes. Her nurturing and empathetic nature makes her a beloved figure who provides comfort and joy to her devotees. Her influence is felt in the healing and transformative power of love, as she encourages those who call upon her to embrace their passions and to seek out meaningful connections. Oshun's ability to create harmony and balance in relationships is a testament to her mastery of the Lover archetype, as she embodies the qualities of compassion and understanding that are essential to healthy relationships.

However, Oshun's intense passion can also lead to challenges. Her desire for admiration and validation can sometimes manifest as vanity or jealousy, reflecting the Lover's shadow side. She must navigate these tendencies to maintain her equilibrium and ensure her connections are genuine and fulfilling. Oshun's journey is a reminder that even the most powerful expressions of love must be balanced with self-awareness and integrity, as true beauty and harmony arise from within.

Path to Individuation
For Oshun, individuation involves balancing her desire for connection and admiration with self-love and personal integrity. By embracing her strengths while remaining aware of her vulnerabilities, Oshun can cultivate relationships that enrich her life without compromising her values. Her journey emphasizes the importance of loving oneself as the foundation for loving others, teaching that true beauty and harmony arise from within. By nurturing her own passions and desires, Oshun can create a life that is both fulfilling and balanced, allowing her love to be a source of inspiration and empowerment.

Oshun's path to individuation is a journey of self-discovery and personal growth, as she learns to channel her passion in ways that are sustainable and enriching. Her story teaches us that the Lover archetype is not only about the pursuit of love but also about the journey toward self-discovery and personal fulfillment. Through Oshun, we learn that the key to fulfilling relationships lies in our ability to love ourselves and to cultivate a rich inner life, allowing our connections to enhance rather than define our identity.

OSHUN STORIES

Oshun's Heroic Sacrifice: The Vulture Transformation
One of the most compelling tales of Oshun in Yoruba mythology is her heroic act of transforming into a vulture to save the world from drought. This story exemplifies her deep compassion and willingness to sacrifice herself for the greater good, reflecting the strength of her connection to humanity and her divine role as a nurturer and protector.

According to the myth, the world was suffering from a severe drought. Rivers had dried up, crops were failing, and people were on the brink of despair. Oshun, known for her close association with water and fertility, realized that drastic action was necessary to save the world from impending disaster. In a selfless act of bravery, she transformed herself into a vulture—a creature capable of soaring to great heights—and flew towards the heavens to plead with Olofin, the supreme deity, for rain.

During her arduous journey, Oshun flew so close to the sun that her feathers were singed, and she lost much of her beauty in the process. Her transformation and ascent are symbolic of the Lover archetype's willingness to endure personal sacrifice for the sake of love and community. By prioritizing the needs of the world over her own, Oshun demonstrated the true power of empathy and dedication. Her efforts were rewarded when Olofin granted her request, bringing rain back to the parched earth and restoring balance to the natural world. This story underscores Oshun's role as a life-giver and healer, emphasizing her dedication to preserving and nurturing life.

This narrative highlights Oshun's strength and heroism, illustrating how the Lover archetype can transcend personal desires to serve the collective good. It also underscores the depth of her connection to humanity and the natural world, showcasing her ability to unite divine intervention with earthly compassion. Through this tale, Oshun exemplifies the potential of the Lover to bring about transformative change, reinforcing the importance of selflessness and empathy in nurturing and protecting others.

Rivalry for Shango's Heart: Beauty, Seduction, and Deceit
In contrast to her heroic tale of sacrifice, another well-known story about Oshun delves into the complexities of love, rivalry, and deception, highlighting the shadow side of the Lover archetype. This narrative involves Oshun's rivalry with Obba Nani and Oya, two other orishas, for the affections of Shango, the orisha of thunder and lightning.

Oshun, renowned for her beauty and charm, sought to win Shango's heart amidst fierce competition from her co-wives. Obba, deeply in love with Shango, sought to please him by following Oshun's deceitful advice. Oshun, driven by jealousy and a desire to eliminate her rival, cunningly suggested to Obba that she could secure Shango's undivided love by offering him a special dish—one that included a piece of her own ear as a token of her devotion.

Believing Oshun's advice, Obba cut off her ear and served it to Shango in his meal. Upon discovering the truth, Shango was horrified and repulsed by Obba's act, leading to her shame and disgrace. This story reveals Oshun's shadow side, where her desire for love and attention leads to manipulation and betrayal, reflecting the darker aspects of the Lover archetype such as vanity, jealousy, and spite.

The rivalry between Oshun, Obba, and Oya also underscores the complexity of relationships and the destructive potential of unchecked passion and jealousy. Oshun's actions, while cunning and ultimately effective in achieving her aims, highlight the Lover's potential to harm others in pursuit of personal desires. This narrative serves as a cautionary tale about the dangers of allowing vanity and jealousy to overshadow empathy and integrity, emphasizing the importance of maintaining balance and self-awareness in relationships.

Despite the deceit and manipulation, Oshun's story with Shango and her rivals ultimately reflects the multifaceted nature of love and attraction, where beauty and seduction are accompanied by challenges and ethical dilemmas. It showcases the Lover archetype's dual potential for both creation and destruction, illustrating the need for mindfulness and ethical consideration in navigating the complexities of love and desire.

These stories about Oshun provide a nuanced portrayal of the Lover archetype, highlighting both its heroic and shadow aspects. Oshun's transformation into a vulture illustrates the power of love and sacrifice, while her rivalry for Shango's affection reveals the potential for manipulation and jealousy. Together, these narratives offer a rich exploration of the complexities of love, illustrating the need for balance, integrity, and self-awareness in nurturing meaningful and harmonious relationships.

EXERCISES & RITUALS

Here are some exercises and rituals designed to align with Oshun and the Lover archetype. These activities focus on overcoming vanity, jealousy, and depression while promoting self-love and self-acceptance.

Mirror Reflection Ritual

<u>Supplies Needed</u>:
- A full-length mirror
- Gold ribbon or fabric
- Candles (preferably gold or yellow)
- A private, comfortable space

<u>Guidelines</u>:
1. Setup: In a private space, wrap the mirror with gold ribbon or fabric, creating a sacred area for reflection. Light the candles around the mirror to create a warm, inviting atmosphere.
2. Reflection Exercise: Stand in front of the mirror and look into your own eyes. Begin by acknowledging and appreciating your unique features and qualities, both physical and emotional.
3. Positive Affirmations: Speak positive affirmations aloud, focusing on self-love and acceptance, such as "I am worthy of love and respect," "I embrace my true self," and "I radiate inner and outer beauty."
4. Release Negative Thoughts: As you gaze into the mirror, identify any negative thoughts or self-criticisms. Imagine them melting away in the candlelight, leaving behind a clearer, more positive self-image.
5. Closing: Finish the ritual by thanking Oshun for her guidance and support. Reflect on the experience and how you can carry these affirmations and insights into your daily life.

<u>Explanation</u>:
This mirror ritual encourages individuals to see themselves through Oshun's loving eyes, fostering self-love and acceptance. By focusing on positive affirmations and releasing negative thoughts, participants can cultivate a more positive self-image and embrace their unique beauty.

Self-Portrait Art Session

Supplies Needed:
- Art supplies (paints, colored pencils, or markers)
- Canvas or paper
- A mirror
- A gold or yellow candle
- A quiet, comfortable space

Guidelines:
1. Setup: Light a gold or yellow candle to invoke Oshun's presence and create a warm, inviting atmosphere. Place a mirror in front of you, ensuring you have a clear view of your face.
2. Intention Setting: Before beginning the self-portrait, set an intention to capture your true essence and beauty. Reflect on the aspects of yourself you wish to honor and embrace during this session.
3. Artistic Exploration: Begin creating your self-portrait, using the mirror as a guide. Focus on representing not just your physical appearance but also the qualities you admire about yourself. Use colors and symbols that resonate with your personality and spirit, such as gold for your inner light or peacock feathers for uniqueness.
4. Reflection: As you work, reflect on the emotions and thoughts that arise. Consider how you perceive yourself and how this exercise might help shift any negative self-perceptions toward a more positive, loving view.
5. Closing: Once completed, place your self-portrait somewhere visible as a reminder of your journey toward self-love and acceptance. Revisit it whenever you need encouragement or affirmation of your worth.

Explanation:
This exercise allows individuals to explore their self-image creatively, encouraging a deeper appreciation for their unique qualities. By focusing on

their essence and inner beauty, participants can foster self-love and diminish feelings of vanity or inadequacy.

Water Cleansing Ritual

Supplies Needed:
- A bowl of water
- Flower petals (yellow or orange are ideal)
- Essential oils (such as orange, jasmine, or ylang-ylang)
- A quiet space for meditation

Guidelines:
1. Setup: In a quiet space, fill a bowl with water and sprinkle in flower petals and a few drops of essential oil. Set the bowl in front of you and sit comfortably.
2. Meditation: Close your eyes and take deep breaths, focusing on the scent and presence of the water before you. Visualize Oshun's rivers flowing around you, cleansing and renewing your spirit.
3. Intention Setting: Place your hands in the water and set an intention to release negative emotions such as jealousy, vanity, or depression. Imagine these feelings flowing out of you and being absorbed by the water.
4. Affirmations: As you touch the water, recite affirmations such as "I release what no longer serves me," "I embrace my true self," and "I am deserving of love and happiness."
5. Closing: When ready, lift your hands from the water and dry them gently, symbolizing the removal of negativity. Dispose of the water outside, returning it to the earth.

Explanation:
This ritual uses the cleansing properties of water, associated with Oshun, to symbolically wash away negative emotions and promote emotional healing.

It reinforces self-acceptance and self-love, providing a fresh start for those seeking to overcome the shadow side of the Lover archetype.

Golden Abundance Ritual

Supplies Needed:
- Gold coins or gold-colored stones
- A small decorative bowl or dish
- Peacocks or peacock feathers (optional)
- Honey
- A quiet space for meditation

Guidelines:
1. Setup: In a quiet space, arrange the gold coins or stones in a decorative bowl. If available, place a peacock feather nearby as a symbol of beauty and abundance.
2. Meditation: Sit comfortably and take a few deep breaths. Visualize Oshun's energy enveloping you, bringing warmth and prosperity.
3. Abundance Affirmations: Hold a gold coin or stone in your hand and recite affirmations focused on abundance and self-worth, such as "I am deserving of all good things," "I attract abundance and love into my life," and "I radiate beauty and confidence."
4. Honey Offering: Dip your finger in honey and taste its sweetness, symbolizing the sweet life Oshun offers. Offer gratitude for your blessings and affirm your commitment to attracting positivity and prosperity.
5. Reflection and Sharing: Share your intentions for abundance and self-love with a trusted friend or community, reinforcing your desires and aligning your energy with Oshun's generous spirit.

Explanation:
This ritual uses gold as a symbol of abundance and prosperity, helping individuals align with Oshun's energy to attract positive experiences and

cultivate a strong sense of self-worth. The inclusion of peacock feathers highlights the uniqueness and beauty inherent in each person, fostering appreciation for one's individuality.

REFLECTIONS

The exploration of Oshun as the embodiment of the Lover archetype offers a profound understanding of the complexities of love, beauty, and connection. Her stories highlight the transformative power of passion and the potential for both creative and destructive expressions of desire. Through her acts of bravery and sacrifice, Oshun demonstrates the profound impact that love and empathy can have on the world, underscoring the importance of balancing personal desires with compassion for others.

As we delve into the multifaceted nature of Oshun, we see the duality inherent in the Lover archetype. Her tales of heroism and sacrifice, such as her selfless act to save the world from drought, illustrate the heights to which love can elevate us. At the same time, her rivalry for Shango's affection reveals the shadow side of the Lover, where jealousy and vanity can lead to manipulation and heartache. These narratives serve as powerful reminders of the need for self-awareness and balance in our pursuit of love and connection.

By embracing the lessons from Oshun's life, individuals can cultivate a deeper appreciation for the beauty and richness of their own experiences. The exercises and rituals associated with Oshun encourage self-reflection, self-love, and a commitment to personal growth. They invite us to explore our own relationship with love, to confront and transform our shadow aspects, and to engage with the world from a place of authenticity and grace.

As we navigate our own paths, let us draw inspiration from Oshun's legacy, striving to embody the Lover's gifts of compassion and creativity while remaining mindful of the potential for excess and imbalance. In doing so, we can foster more harmonious relationships with ourselves and others, allowing the energy of love to guide us toward a more fulfilling and interconnected existence.

Chapter 10

The Creator

The Creator archetype in Jungian psychology embodies the fundamental drive to bring new ideas, forms, and worlds into existence. This archetype is characterized by boundless creativity, imagination, and the vision to transform raw materials into something entirely new. The Creator is not only an artist or inventor but also a visionary capable of perceiving potential where others see nothing but limitations. This archetype's essence lies in the ability to innovate, to envision possibilities beyond the ordinary, and to manifest those visions into reality.

The Creator archetype is marked by a deep-seated need to express individuality through the creation of something that resonates with both personal and universal meaning. Whether through art, literature, science, or any form of creative endeavor, the Creator seeks to leave a lasting impact on the world. This drive to create often stems from a profound connection to the inner world of imagination and a desire to bring forth what lies within into the external world. The Creator archetype, therefore, is a bridge between the internal and external realms, turning thoughts and ideas into tangible reality.

However, the Creator's journey is not without challenges. The same qualities that fuel their creativity—imagination, innovation, and vision—can also lead to potential pitfalls. The Creator's intense focus on their vision may result in perfectionism, where the pursuit of an ideal becomes an obstacle to completion and satisfaction. Additionally, the Creator may struggle with self-doubt and the fear of failure, particularly when their creations do not meet their high standards or when they encounter resistance from others. To thrive, the Creator must learn to navigate these challenges, balancing their visionary aspirations with practical considerations and embracing the imperfections inherent in the creative process.

Characteristics and Traits
The Creator archetype is defined by its emphasis on creativity, imagination, and vision. Creators possess an innate ability to envision possibilities and to see the world through a lens of potential and transformation. They are often innovators and pioneers, unafraid to explore new ideas and push boundaries. This archetype thrives on originality and self-expression, driven by the desire to manifest their unique perspectives in the world.

Creators are characterized by their ability to think outside the box and to approach problems with fresh, innovative solutions. They have a keen sense of aesthetics and are often drawn to beauty and harmony, whether in the arts, sciences, or everyday life. The Creator archetype values authenticity and seeks to create work that is a true reflection of their inner self. This commitment to authenticity often results in creations that resonate deeply with others, inspiring and challenging them to see the world in new ways.

However, the Creator's visionary outlook can sometimes lead to challenges. Their pursuit of perfection may cause them to become overly critical of their work, hindering their ability to complete projects or to share their creations with the world. The Creator may also experience frustration when their visions are not realized as they imagined or when they face external criticism or obstacles. To overcome these challenges, Creators must cultivate resilience and adaptability, learning to accept the imperfections of their work and to embrace the process of creation as much as the end result.

Strengths and Weaknesses
The strengths of the Creator archetype are rooted in their ability to inspire and innovate. Creators are visionaries who can see beyond the status quo and imagine new possibilities, often leading to groundbreaking discoveries and advancements. Their creativity fuels progress and change, allowing them to contribute significantly to their fields and to society as a whole. The Creator's dedication to self-expression and authenticity also inspires others to embrace their own creative potential, fostering a culture of innovation and exploration.

However, the Creator's strengths can also give rise to weaknesses. The pursuit of perfection and the relentless drive to achieve their vision can lead to burnout and frustration. Creators may struggle with self-doubt, fearing that their work is not good enough or that it will not be appreciated by others. This fear of failure can hinder their ability to take risks and to share their creations with the world. Additionally, the Creator's focus on their vision may lead to an imbalance in their personal lives, as they prioritize their creative pursuits over other responsibilities or relationships.

To navigate these challenges, Creators must learn to balance their visionary aspirations with practical considerations. Embracing the iterative nature of the creative process and allowing for imperfections can help them overcome the fear of failure and self-doubt. By cultivating a mindset of curiosity and openness, Creators can continue to innovate and inspire while maintaining a healthy balance between their creative endeavors and other aspects of their lives.

Cultural Examples
The Creator archetype is prevalent across cultures, often depicted as artists, inventors, and pioneers who transform the world through their creative

vision. In literature and mythology, figures such as Leonardo da Vinci and Nikola Tesla exemplify the Creator archetype. Leonardo da Vinci's contributions to art and science showcase his boundless creativity and imagination, while Nikola Tesla's inventions and innovations demonstrate his visionary approach to transforming the world through technology.

In mythology, Prometheus, the Titan who brought fire to humanity, symbolizes the Creator's drive to innovate and empower others through knowledge and invention. Prometheus's act of defiance and his willingness to challenge the gods to bring progress to humanity highlight the Creator's role as a catalyst for change and transformation. Similarly, figures like Hephaestus, the Greek god of craftsmanship, embody the Creator's ability to shape and mold materials into new forms, reflecting the transformative power of creativity.

In contemporary culture, the Creator archetype is evident in individuals who push the boundaries of their fields, from artists and musicians to scientists and entrepreneurs. Figures such as Steve Jobs and J.K. Rowling illustrate the Creator's influence, demonstrating how creativity and vision can lead to groundbreaking innovations and cultural shifts. These cultural examples highlight the Creator's impact on society, emphasizing the importance of imagination and innovation in shaping the world.

Historical or Contemporary Figures
Leonardo da Vinci (1452–1519)
Leonardo da Vinci, the Italian polymath, is a quintessential example of the Creator archetype. Da Vinci's mastery in art, science, and invention embodies the Creator's drive to bring ideas to life and push the boundaries of creativity. His works, such as the "Mona Lisa" and "The Last Supper," along with his numerous scientific sketches, demonstrate the Creator's vision and innovation.

Frida Kahlo (1907–1954)
Frida Kahlo, the Mexican painter, also represents the Creator archetype. Kahlo's deeply personal and symbolic works, often exploring themes of identity, pain, and resilience, reflect the Creator's ability to transform inner experiences into powerful artistic expressions. Her unique style and unapologetic self-expression have made her an enduring icon of creativity.

In Psychology
In modern psychology, the Creator archetype is associated with the process of individuation and self-actualization. This archetype encourages individuals to explore their creative potential and to use their talents to shape their lives and the world around them. Creative therapies, such as art therapy and music therapy, draw on the Creator archetype's energy to help individuals express their emotions and experiences in transformative ways. The Creator's influence is also evident in the growing emphasis on personal branding and the idea that individuals can craft their own identities and destinies through creative self-expression.

Shadow Side
The shadow side of the Creator archetype can manifest in various ways, often stemming from the challenges associated with the pursuit of perfection and the fear of failure. Creators may become overly focused on their vision, leading to obsessive tendencies and an inability to accept imperfections. This drive for perfection can result in frustration and burnout, as Creators push themselves to meet impossibly high standards or struggle to bring their ideas to fruition.

The shadow side of the Creator also includes the potential for isolation, as the intense focus on creative pursuits may lead to neglect of personal relationships or responsibilities. Creators may become so absorbed in their work that they lose sight of the world around them, leading to feelings of disconnect or alienation. Additionally, the fear of criticism or rejection may prevent Creators from sharing their work with others, limiting their ability to connect and collaborate.

To address the shadow side of the Creator, individuals must cultivate self-awareness and balance. Embracing the iterative nature of the creative process and accepting imperfections can help Creators overcome self-doubt and perfectionism. By fostering resilience and adaptability, Creators can navigate the challenges of the creative journey while maintaining a healthy balance between their visionary aspirations and the realities of life.

Path to Individuation
The path to individuation for the Creator archetype involves integrating creativity with practicality and learning to accept the imperfections inherent in the creative process. This journey requires cultivating self-awareness and embracing collaboration, recognizing that true innovation often arises from the interplay of diverse perspectives and ideas. By balancing their visionary aspirations with practical considerations, Creators can achieve a harmonious integration of their creative energies, allowing their unique talents to flourish.

For Creators, individuation is about finding harmony between their inner vision and the external world. This involves embracing the iterative nature of creation and recognizing that failure and setbacks are part of the journey toward innovation and growth. By fostering a mindset of curiosity and openness, Creators can continue to explore new ideas and push boundaries while remaining grounded in reality.

The Creator's path to individuation also emphasizes the importance of self-care and balance. By prioritizing their well-being and maintaining a healthy balance between their creative pursuits and other aspects of their lives, Creators can sustain their energy and passion over the long term. Through this process, Creators can achieve a sense of fulfillment and purpose, realizing their potential to shape and transform the world.

THE CREATOR

ORISHAOKO AS THE CREATOR

Orishaoko, the orisha of agriculture, fertility, and the earth, embodies the Creator archetype through his deep connection to the land and his role in sustaining life. As the deity responsible for the fertility of the earth and the abundance of the harvest, Orishaoko is a powerful symbol of creation and renewal, guiding the cycles of growth and transformation that define the natural world.

While Orishaoko may be an unconventional choice for the Creator archetype, given the myriad other worthy candidates among the orisha, I chose him for this role not only because he is suitable but also because he is frequently overlooked. His profound relationship with the earth and its cycles of growth highlights his creative powers and ability to nurture and sustain life. Orishaoko's embodiment of the Creator archetype encourages us to honor the creative forces within ourselves and recognize the interconnectedness of all life.

Through Orishaoko, we are reminded of the Creator's capacity to bring forth abundance and transformation, urging us to embrace our own creative potential and engage deeply with the world around us. His presence as the Creator serves as a powerful testament to the importance of recognizing and valuing those often hidden from the spotlight, emphasizing that true creativity and influence can come from the most unexpected places.

Connection to the Creator Archetype
Orishaoko's primary role as the orisha of agriculture aligns with the Creator's focus on bringing new life and forms into existence. His influence over the land and its fertility underscores his connection to the processes of creation and renewal, highlighting the transformative power of nature. Orishaoko embodies the Creator's drive to shape the world and to nurture the growth and development of all living things, serving as a guardian of the earth's resources and a steward of its bounty.

Orishaoko's role in agriculture and fertility involves the innovation and knowledge required to cultivate the land successfully. This includes understanding the rhythms of nature and adapting to environmental changes, which are essential traits of the Creator archetype. His ability to foster growth and abundance ensures the prosperity and well-being of his community, reflecting the Creator's strengths in inspiring and nurturing life.

Strengths and Weaknesses
As a Creator, Orishaoko's strengths lie in his ability to provide sustenance and to foster growth and abundance. His deep understanding of the earth's rhythms and cycles allows him to innovate and adapt, using his knowledge to cultivate the land and to support the flourishing of life. However, Orishaoko's commitment to creation and productivity can also lead to challenges, such as an overemphasis on outcomes or a tendency to prioritize work over rest and rejuvenation. The Creator must learn to balance their drive for innovation with the need for sustainability and balance, ensuring that their creative endeavors are both fruitful and sustainable.

Orishaoko's strengths as a Creator include his capacity to inspire and to bring about change. His role as a provider and nurturer highlights his ability to support and sustain life, fostering a sense of community and interconnectedness. However, the Creator's focus on productivity and outcomes may lead to stress or burnout, as Orishaoko strives to meet the demands of the harvest and to ensure the land's fertility. To navigate these challenges, Orishaoko must cultivate resilience and adaptability, learning to balance his visionary aspirations with the practicalities of execution.

Cultural Significance
In Yoruba culture and its diasporic traditions, Orishaoko is revered as a guardian of the land and a symbol of fertility and abundance. His rituals often involve celebrations of the harvest and gratitude for the earth's bounty, emphasizing the importance of harmony and balance in the relationship

between humanity and nature. Orishaoko's teachings highlight the interconnectedness of all life and the importance of nurturing and sustaining the earth's resources for future generations.

Orishaoko's role in Yoruba culture emphasizes the significance of living in harmony with nature and respecting the earth's resources. His teachings on agriculture and fertility offer valuable lessons in sustainability and stewardship, aligning with the Creator archetype's focus on creativity, innovation, and vision. Through his example, Orishaoko inspires individuals to embrace their own creative potential and to cultivate a deeper understanding of the interconnectedness of life and the natural world.

Shadow Side
The shadow side of Orishaoko, as with any Creator archetype, emerges when the desire for creation becomes obsessive or when the pursuit of perfection leads to rigidity and inflexibility. Orishaoko's focus on productivity and outcomes can sometimes result in stress or burnout, as he strives to meet the demands of the harvest and to ensure the land's fertility. This shadow aspect serves as a reminder of the importance of self-care and balance in the creative process, emphasizing the need for patience and adaptability in the face of challenges.

The shadow side of Orishaoko also includes the potential for isolation, as the intense focus on creative pursuits may lead to neglect of personal relationships or responsibilities. Orishaoko may become so absorbed in his work that he loses sight of the world around him, leading to feelings of disconnect or alienation. Additionally, the fear of criticism or rejection may prevent Orishaoko from sharing his work with others, limiting his ability to connect and collaborate.

Path to Individuation
For Orishaoko, the path to individuation involves embracing his role as a creator while also recognizing the importance of rest and renewal. This

journey requires cultivating self-awareness and learning to balance his drive for productivity with the need for reflection and rejuvenation. By fostering a deep connection to the earth and its cycles, Orishaoko can achieve a harmonious integration of his creative energies, allowing him to nurture and sustain life in a way that is both fulfilling and sustainable.

Orishaoko's path to individuation emphasizes the importance of balance and self-care in the creative process. By prioritizing his well-being and maintaining a healthy balance between his creative pursuits and other aspects of his life, Orishaoko can sustain his energy and passion over the long term. Through this process, Orishaoko can achieve a sense of fulfillment and purpose, realizing his potential to shape and transform the world.

Orishaoko's alignment with the Creator archetype offers valuable insights into the dynamics of creation and the importance of nurturing and sustaining life. His connection to the earth and his dedication to providing for his community exemplify the qualities of creativity, innovation, and vision that define the Creator. Through his teachings, Orishaoko inspires individuals to embrace their own creative potential and to cultivate a deeper understanding of the interconnectedness of life and the natural world.

ORISHAOKO STORIES

In the Yoruba pantheon, Orishaoko stands as a testament to the power of fertility, agriculture, and the earth. As the orisha responsible for the cultivation of crops and the fertility of the land, Orishaoko embodies the Creator archetype through his nurturing and generative capabilities. His stories, deeply embedded in Yoruba mythology, highlight both the positive and negative aspects of this archetype, illustrating the complex interplay between creation, sustenance, and human ambition.

The Fertility of the Land

One of the most celebrated stories of Orishaoko involves his role in ensuring the fertility of the earth and the abundance of the harvest. In Yoruba mythology, Orishaoko is revered for his ability to bring life to barren lands, transforming desolate fields into thriving gardens. This narrative underscores the Creator archetype's qualities of imagination, vision, and the transformative power of creation. Orishaoko's influence over agriculture is not merely about producing crops but about nurturing the land and fostering an environment where life can flourish.

In this tale, Orishaoko travels across the lands, blessing the fields and imparting his wisdom to farmers. He teaches them the secrets of agriculture, sharing his knowledge of the seasons, soil, and the rhythms of nature. Through his guidance, barren lands become fertile, and the people celebrate bountiful harvests. This story highlights Orishaoko's positive aspects as a Creator: his generosity, his connection to the natural world, and his ability to inspire growth and abundance.

However, this story also alludes to the challenges inherent in the Creator archetype. The responsibility of ensuring fertility and abundance can lead to pressure and stress, particularly when environmental conditions are unfavorable. Orishaoko's deep connection to the land means that he experiences the triumphs and failures of the harvest as a personal reflection of his abilities. This narrative serves as a reminder of the importance of balance and the need to embrace both success and failure as part of the creative process.

The Conflict of Innovation

Another well-known story involving Orishaoko centers on his innovation in agricultural practices, a tale that underscores both the strengths and weaknesses of the Creator archetype. In this story, Orishaoko introduces a new method of planting that promises to double the yield of the crops. The farmers, eager for prosperity, quickly adopt his technique, and initially, the results are astounding. The fields overflow with abundance, and the people praise Orishaoko for his genius.

Yet, as time passes, the soil becomes depleted, and the crops begin to fail. The farmers, having relied too heavily on the new method, face hardship and scarcity. In his zeal for innovation, Orishaoko overlooked the long-term sustainability of his approach, leading to unintended consequences. This tale illustrates the Creator's potential for shortsightedness, where the pursuit of innovation can overshadow practical considerations and lead to negative outcomes.

Through this story, Orishaoko learns the importance of balance and sustainability. He realizes that true creation is not just about immediate results but about fostering a harmonious relationship with the earth that ensures ongoing fertility and abundance. The lesson here is that innovation must be tempered with wisdom and foresight, reflecting the Creator's journey toward individuation and the integration of creativity with responsibility.

The Sacred Grove
The story of Orishaoko's sacred grove further explores his role as a protector and nurturer of the earth, highlighting the Creator's dual aspects of creativity and stewardship. According to Yoruba legend, Orishaoko tends to a sacred grove that serves as a sanctuary for the spirits of the land. This grove, lush with life and beauty, is a testament to Orishaoko's power to nurture and protect the natural world.

The sacred grove is a place of refuge and healing, where those seeking guidance and renewal can connect with the earth and its energies. Orishaoko's role as a guardian of this space reflects the Creator's responsibility to preserve and sustain the creations brought into existence. The grove symbolizes the interconnectedness of all life and the Creator's duty to honor and protect the environment that supports their creations.

THE CREATOR

Yet, the story also reveals the challenges faced by Orishaoko as a steward of the land. The sacred grove is threatened by those who seek to exploit its resources for personal gain, reflecting the darker aspects of human ambition and greed. Orishaoko must defend the grove, balancing his nurturing instincts with the need to protect and preserve. This conflict illustrates the Creator's struggle to maintain integrity and purpose in the face of external pressures, emphasizing the importance of resilience and commitment to one's ideals.

Through these stories, Orishaoko embodies the Creator archetype's complexities, showcasing both the positive and negative aspects of creation. His tales offer insights into the creative journey, highlighting the importance of balance, sustainability, and the harmonious integration of vision and responsibility. By aligning with Orishaoko's energy, individuals can embrace their own creative potential while cultivating a deeper connection to the earth and the cycles of life.

EXERCISES & RITUALS

Here are some exercises and rituals designed to align with Orishaoko and the Creator Archetype. These activities focus on promoting rest, rejuvenation, and balance while overcoming stress and burnout. They also encourage individuals to embrace their creative potential and deepen their connection with the natural world.

Garden of Ideas Ritual

Supplies Needed:
- Small potted plant or garden plot
- Seeds or seedlings
- Gardening tools
- Notebook and pen for journaling

Guidelines:
1. Preparation: Choose a small area in your garden or a potted plant for your ritual. Gather seeds or seedlings and any necessary gardening tools.
2. Intention Setting: Before planting, set an intention for your creative growth. Consider what projects or ideas you wish to cultivate and how you can nurture them.
3. Planting: Plant your seeds or seedlings, focusing on the act of creation and the potential for growth. As you plant, visualize your creative ideas taking root and flourishing.
4. Care and Nurturing: Commit to caring for your plants regularly, using the act of gardening as a metaphor for nurturing your creativity. Reflect on the patience and dedication required to foster growth.
5. Journaling and Reflection: Use your notebook to track the progress of your plants and your creative endeavors. Reflect on the lessons learned from the natural world and how they apply to your creative journey.

Explanation:
This ritual uses gardening as a metaphor for nurturing creativity and overcoming stress. By aligning with Orishaoko's energy, individuals can cultivate a sense of patience and perseverance, allowing their creative ideas to grow and flourish alongside their plants.

Vision Board for Creative Balance

Supplies Needed:
- Poster board or large piece of paper
- Magazines or printed images
- Scissors, glue, markers
- Optional: natural elements (leaves, flowers, etc.)

THE CREATOR

<u>Guidelines</u>:
1. Preparation: Gather your supplies and find a comfortable space to create your vision board. Choose images and words that resonate with your creative aspirations and desires for balance and rejuvenation.
2. Intention Setting: Set an intention for your vision board, focusing on the areas of your life where you seek creative growth and balance. Consider what you wish to cultivate and how you can nurture your creative energies.
3. Creating the Vision Board: Begin arranging your images and words on the board, using markers and natural elements to enhance your creation. Focus on the themes of creativity, rest, and rejuvenation as you work.
4. Reflection and Integration: Once your vision board is complete, take time to reflect on the themes and ideas you have chosen. Consider how you can integrate these insights into your daily life and creative pursuits.
5. Display and Engagement: Place your vision board somewhere visible as a reminder of your creative goals and intentions. Revisit it regularly to reinforce your commitment to balance and rejuvenation.

<u>Explanation</u>:
Creating a vision board encourages individuals to clarify their creative goals and aspirations, promoting balance and rejuvenation. By aligning with Orishaoko's energy, participants can cultivate a deeper understanding of their creative potential and the interconnectedness of life and the natural world.

Earth Mandala Creation

<u>Supplies Needed</u>:
- Natural materials (leaves, flowers, stones, seeds)

- Open outdoor space
- Optional: camera or smartphone for documentation

Guidelines:
1. Preparation: Gather natural materials such as leaves, flowers, stones, and seeds from your surroundings. Find an open outdoor space where you can create your mandala.
2. Intention Setting: Set an intention for your mandala creation, focusing on the themes of harmony, balance, and interconnectedness. Consider what you wish to express through your design.
3. Creating the Mandala: Begin arranging the natural materials in a circular pattern, allowing your creativity to guide you. Focus on symmetry and balance, using the materials to reflect the beauty and abundance of the earth.
4. Mindful Engagement: As you create, remain present and mindful of your connection to the earth and its elements. Consider how each piece contributes to the whole and how this reflects your own creative journey.
5. Reflection and Documentation: Once your mandala is complete, spend a few moments reflecting on its significance. Consider documenting your creation with a photo to capture the moment and to inspire future creative endeavors.

Explanation:
Creating an earth mandala allows individuals to connect with the natural world and to express their creativity through the use of natural materials. By aligning with Orishaoko's energy, participants can embrace the harmony and balance inherent in nature and reflect this in their creative pursuits.

Seasonal Feast and Celebration

Supplies Needed:

- Seasonal produce and ingredients
- Cooking utensils and equipment
- Table for dining and sharing

Guidelines:
1. Preparation: Gather fresh, seasonal produce and ingredients for your feast, focusing on items that reflect the current harvest. Plan a menu that celebrates the abundance of the earth and the creativity involved in preparing a meal.
2. Intention Setting: Set an intention for celebration and gratitude for the earth's bounty. Consider the creativity and collaboration involved in preparing and sharing a meal.
3. Cooking and Creativity: Engage in the creative process of cooking, exploring new recipes and techniques. Focus on the flavors and textures of the ingredients, allowing your creativity to guide you in crafting a delicious and nourishing meal.
4. Sharing and Community: Invite family or friends to join you in the feast, sharing the meal and the gratitude for the earth's abundance. Reflect on the connections formed through food and the role of the earth in sustaining life.
5. Reflection and Gratitude: After the meal, spend time reflecting on the experience and the creative journey involved in preparing and sharing the feast. Consider how the celebration of the earth's abundance can inspire future creative endeavors.

Explanation:

A seasonal feast and celebration highlight the creativity and collaboration involved in preparing and sharing a meal. By aligning with Orishaoko's energy, participants can deepen their appreciation for the earth's bounty and the interconnectedness of life.

REFLECTIONS

Exploring Orishaoko as the embodiment of the Creator archetype provides a profound understanding of the dynamics of creativity, growth, and sustenance. Through his stories and attributes, Orishaoko reveals the essential qualities of vision, imagination, and the nurturing power necessary for creation. His connection to the earth and his role in ensuring the fertility and abundance of the land underscore the Creator's capacity to bring forth life and transform environments.

Orishaoko's narratives remind us of the delicate balance between innovation and sustainability, emphasizing the need for creators to remain mindful of the long-term impact of their endeavors. His journey highlights the importance of resilience and adaptability, encouraging individuals to embrace challenges as opportunities for growth and learning. By aligning with Orishaoko's energy, creators can cultivate a deeper connection to the natural world, drawing inspiration from the earth's cycles and rhythms.

The lessons from Orishaoko's stories resonate with the universal themes of creation and renewal, offering valuable insights into the complexities of the creative process. As individuals engage with the Creator archetype, they are invited to explore their own potential for innovation and expression, finding harmony between their inner vision and the external world. Orishaoko's example inspires a commitment to nurturing and sustaining life, reminding us of the transformative power of creativity and its capacity to shape and enrich our lives.

Chapter 11

The Jester

The Jester archetype is defined by its vibrant energy, humor, and the ability to bring joy to those around it. Known for their playful nature and penchant for mischief, Jesters are often seen as the life of the party, using their wit and charm to entertain and lighten the mood. Their humor can be a powerful tool, capable of disarming tension and fostering connection. Jesters are adept at finding joy in everyday life, and their optimism and enthusiasm are infectious. They remind others of the importance of living in the moment, encouraging spontaneity and creativity.

Jesters possess a unique perspective that allows them to see the world from a different angle. This ability to view situations through a lens of humor and playfulness often provides them with insights that others might overlook. They have a knack for pointing out absurdities and contradictions, using humor to highlight truths and provoke thought. Jesters can be both entertainers and philosophers, using their humor to inspire and challenge conventional thinking.

However, the Jester's focus on humor and play can sometimes lead to a disregard for responsibility and seriousness. While their levity is a strength, it can also become a weakness if it leads to avoidance or a lack of accountability. Balancing their playful nature with a sense of responsibility is a key aspect of the Jester archetype's journey toward individuation.

Strengths and Weaknesses
The Jester archetype's strengths lie in its ability to uplift and inspire others through humor and joy. Jesters have a natural talent for making people laugh and feel at ease, creating a positive atmosphere wherever they go. Their playful nature encourages creativity and innovation, fostering an environment where new ideas can flourish. Jesters also possess a unique ability to diffuse tension and conflict, using humor to bridge divides and bring people together.

Jesters are often seen as agents of change, using their humor to challenge the status quo and question societal norms. Their ability to see the world from a different perspective allows them to offer fresh insights and encourage others to think outside the box. Jesters are not afraid to take risks or push boundaries, making them catalysts for transformation and growth.

However, the Jester's strengths can also become weaknesses if not balanced with a sense of responsibility. Their focus on humor and play can sometimes lead to avoidance of serious issues or a lack of commitment to long-term goals. Jesters may struggle with maintaining consistency and discipline, as their desire for fun and excitement can sometimes overshadow their obligations. Additionally, their penchant for mischief can sometimes lead to trouble, as they may push boundaries too far or fail to consider the consequences of their actions.

To overcome these challenges, Jesters must learn to balance their playful nature with a sense of responsibility and accountability. By embracing their strengths while also acknowledging their weaknesses, Jesters can navigate their journey toward individuation with greater awareness and purpose.

Cultural Examples
The Jester archetype is prevalent in literature, film, and mythology, often portrayed as characters who use humor and wit to navigate the world. These characters are often seen as both entertainers and truth-tellers, using their humor to challenge authority and provoke thought.

One classic example of the Jester archetype is Shakespeare's character Falstaff from *Henry IV*. Falstaff is a larger-than-life figure known for his wit, humor, and love of indulgence. His playful antics and humorous commentary provide comic relief while also offering insights into the complexities of human nature and the challenges of leadership. Despite his flaws, Falstaff's humor and charisma make him a beloved character, embodying the Jester's ability to entertain and enlighten.

In modern literature, the character of the Joker in the Batman series serves as a darker representation of the Jester archetype. While the Joker's humor is often malevolent and destructive, he embodies the Jester's role as a disruptor and provocateur. His chaotic nature and penchant for mischief challenge the established order, highlighting the Jester's potential to subvert and transform.

In mythology, the Norse god Loki exemplifies the Jester archetype. Known for his cunning and trickery, Loki uses his wit and humor to manipulate events and challenge the gods. His actions often lead to unexpected consequences, reflecting the Jester's ability to disrupt and reshape the world.

These cultural examples illustrate the multifaceted nature of the Jester archetype, highlighting its potential for both positive and negative expression. By exploring these narratives, we gain a deeper understanding of the Jester's role in society and its impact on the human experience.

Historical or Contemporary Figures
Charlie Chaplin (1889–1977)
Charlie Chaplin, the English comic actor and filmmaker, epitomizes the Jester archetype through his work in silent film, particularly his iconic character "The Tramp." Chaplin's humor, often combined with social and political commentary, used the Jester's power to entertain, challenge norms, and provoke thought. His ability to make audiences laugh while addressing serious issues underscores the Jester's role in society.

Robin Williams (1951–2014)
Robin Williams, the American actor and comedian, also embodies the Jester archetype. Known for his quick wit, improvisational skills, and ability to bring joy to others, Williams used humor as a means of connection and healing. His performances, both comedic and dramatic, reveal the depth of the Jester archetype, showcasing how humor can be a powerful tool for exploring the human condition.

In Psychology
The Jester archetype is also significant in modern psychology, where it is associated with the therapeutic use of humor and playfulness. Laughter therapy, for example, draws on the Jester archetype's energy to promote healing and well-being, helping individuals to reduce stress, build resilience, and foster positive social connections. The Jester's influence is also evident in the rise of improvisational comedy and other forms of creative expression that encourage spontaneity, creativity, and joy. This archetype reminds us of the importance of humor in maintaining a balanced perspective on life, as well as the power of laughter to bring people together and to effect change.

Shadow Side
The shadow side of the Jester archetype manifests when humor and playfulness are used to avoid or mask deeper issues. Jesters may use humor as a defense mechanism, deflecting attention from their own vulnerabilities

or the seriousness of a situation. This avoidance can lead to a lack of accountability, as Jesters may struggle to confront difficult emotions or address important responsibilities.

The Jester's focus on levity can also result in a superficial approach to life, where meaningful connections and goals are overshadowed by the pursuit of fun and excitement. This can lead to a sense of aimlessness or a lack of fulfillment, as Jesters may find themselves constantly seeking the next thrill without considering the long-term consequences of their actions.

Additionally, the Jester's penchant for mischief can sometimes lead to destructive behavior. When boundaries are pushed too far, the Jester's actions can harm themselves or others, leading to regret and isolation. This shadow side highlights the importance of balance and self-awareness, as Jesters must learn to channel their energy positively and constructively.

To address the shadow side of the Jester archetype, individuals must cultivate a sense of responsibility and purpose. By acknowledging their vulnerabilities and embracing the importance of meaningful connections, Jesters can transcend the limitations of their archetype and achieve a more balanced and fulfilling life.

Path to Individuation

The path to individuation for the Jester archetype involves integrating their playful nature with a sense of responsibility and purpose. Jesters must learn to balance their desire for fun and excitement with their obligations and commitments, ensuring that their actions align with their values and goals.

One aspect of the individuation process for Jesters is cultivating self-awareness and mindfulness. By becoming more attuned to their thoughts, emotions, and actions, Jesters can gain insight into their motivations and the impact of their behavior. This self-awareness allows them to make more conscious choices and to channel their energy in ways that are both joyful and productive.

Jesters must also learn to embrace the importance of meaningful connections and long-term goals. By fostering relationships based on trust and authenticity, Jesters can create a supportive network that encourages growth and transformation. Setting goals that align with their values and passions allows Jesters to find fulfillment beyond the pursuit of momentary pleasure, creating a sense of purpose and direction.

Finally, Jesters must learn to embrace the transformative power of humor and play while recognizing the importance of balance and responsibility. By integrating these qualities, Jesters can navigate their journey toward individuation with greater awareness and intention, using their unique perspective to inspire and uplift those around them.

ELEGUA AS THE JESTER

Elegua, a prominent orisha in the Yoruba pantheon, embodies the Jester archetype through his playful nature, humor, and role as a trickster and guide. Known as the keeper of crossroads and the messenger between worlds, Elegua is revered for his ability to open doors, remove obstacles, and bring joy and laughter to those he encounters.

Connection to the Jester Archetype
Elegua's playful nature and love of mischief make him a quintessential embodiment of the Jester archetype. He is often depicted as a child or a young man, symbolizing his youthful energy and zest for life. Elegua's humor and wit are central to his identity, and he uses these qualities to navigate the world and to interact with both humans and other orisha.

Elegua is known for his role as a trickster, using his cunning and cleverness to challenge authority and disrupt the status quo. His actions often serve as

THE JESTER

lessons or tests, encouraging individuals to think critically and to embrace the unexpected. Elegua's playful antics and unpredictable nature reflect the Jester's ability to inspire creativity and transformation.

Strengths and Weaknesses

Elegua's strengths as the Jester archetype are evident in his ability to uplift and inspire others through humor and play. His presence brings joy and laughter, creating a positive atmosphere that encourages spontaneity and innovation. Elegua's role as a guide and protector underscores his importance within the Yoruba pantheon, as he helps individuals navigate the complexities of life and find their path.

However, Elegua's penchant for mischief can also become a weakness if not balanced with responsibility. His trickster nature can sometimes lead to chaos or confusion, as his actions may have unintended consequences. To overcome these challenges, Elegua must learn to balance his playful nature with a sense of accountability and purpose.

Cultural Significance

Elegua holds significant cultural importance within Yoruba religion and its diasporic adaptations. He is often invoked at the beginning of rituals and ceremonies, as his blessing is essential for success and protection. Elegua's role as a mediator between worlds highlights his importance as a guide and messenger, bridging the gap between the physical and spiritual realms.

In addition to his religious significance, Elegua is a symbol of resilience and adaptability. His ability to navigate different worlds and to use humor as a tool for transformation reflects the Jester's role as a catalyst for change. Elegua's narratives offer valuable lessons on the power of humor and the importance of embracing life's uncertainties.

Shadow Side
The shadow side of Elegua's story is reflected in his trickster nature and the potential for mischief to lead to chaos or harm. While Elegua's actions are often intended to teach or guide, they can sometimes result in confusion or disruption. This aspect of Elegua's character highlights the importance of balance and self-awareness, as he must learn to channel his energy positively and constructively.

Elegua's journey underscores the potential for humor to become a defense mechanism, masking deeper issues or avoiding responsibility. To navigate the shadow side of the Jester archetype, Elegua must cultivate self-awareness and embrace the importance of accountability and purpose.

Path to Individuation
Elegua's path to individuation involves integrating his playful nature with a sense of responsibility and purpose. By embracing his role as a guide and protector, Elegua can channel his energy in ways that uplift and inspire others. His journey highlights the importance of balance, self-awareness, and meaningful connections, allowing him to transcend the limitations of the Jester archetype.

Through his narratives, Elegua teaches the value of humor and playfulness while emphasizing the need for accountability and purpose. By aligning with the Jester archetype with intention and awareness, individuals can cultivate a life of joy, creativity, and transformation.

ELEGUA STORIES

Elegua, the quintessential trickster orisha in Yoruba mythology, is renowned for his cunning, humor, and ability to create chaos as a means of imparting wisdom. His stories are rich with lessons about perspective, understanding, and the consequences of human folly. Below are some of the most well-known tales that highlight Elegua's trickster nature and his role as a teacher of life's unpredictable paths.

Elegua and the Two Friends

One of the most famous stories about Elegua involves his decision to test the bond between two friends. Elegua dressed himself in a garment that was half red and half black and walked down the road between the two friends, who were working in adjacent fields. As Elegua passed between them, he ensured that each friend saw only one color of his attire. Later, when the two friends met, they began discussing the strange man they had seen. One insisted that the man was dressed in red, while the other was adamant that he wore black. The argument escalated into a heated quarrel, with each friend unwilling to concede the other's point of view.

Elegua, watching from a distance, revealed himself and explained how he had walked between them wearing a garment of two colors. This revelation brought the friends to the realization that their perspectives were limited by their vantage points. The lesson Elegua imparted was clear: truth can be multifaceted, and understanding another's perspective is crucial for maintaining harmony and avoiding conflict. This story underscores Elegua's role as a mediator and teacher, using his trickery to illuminate deeper truths about human nature and relationships.

Elegua and the Farmer's Misfortune

Another tale that showcases Elegua's trickster nature involves a farmer who was experiencing a string of bad luck. The farmer, frustrated with his misfortune, decided to make an offering to Elegua, hoping for a change in his circumstances. Elegua, always unpredictable, decided to test the farmer's sincerity and patience.

Elegua appeared to the farmer in disguise and instructed him to plant his crops in a particular manner, promising that his fortune would improve if he followed the instructions precisely. The farmer, desperate for change, obeyed Elegua's directions but became impatient as the days passed without any visible improvement.

Growing restless, the farmer decided to abandon Elegua's instructions, believing that they were ineffective. Shortly after, Elegua visited the farmer once more, revealing his true identity and admonishing the farmer for his impatience and lack of faith. Elegua then instructed him to follow the original plan again, this time with perseverance. When the farmer did so, his fields flourished, and his fortune was restored.

This story illustrates Elegua's role as a teacher of patience and faith, demonstrating that persistence and trust in divine guidance can lead to eventual success. Elegua's trickery, in this case, served as a lesson in the virtues of patience and belief.

Elegua and the Crossroads
Elegua is often associated with crossroads, representing the choices and possibilities that life presents. In one tale, a traveler arrived at a crossroads and was unsure which path to take. Elegua, observing from a distance, decided to present the traveler with a challenge.

Disguised as a beggar, Elegua approached the traveler and offered advice, suggesting that one path led to fortune while the other to misfortune. However, Elegua's cryptic directions were deliberately misleading, designed to test the traveler's intuition and decision-making skills.

The traveler, confused by the conflicting advice, realized that he needed to rely on his own instincts rather than external guidance. After careful reflection, he chose a path that ultimately led to a rewarding outcome. Elegua, pleased with the traveler's decision, revealed himself and praised the traveler for his discernment and courage.

THE JESTER

This story highlights Elegua's role as a guardian of crossroads and choices, teaching individuals to trust their instincts and to make decisions based on inner wisdom. Elegua's challenge emphasizes the importance of self-reliance and personal growth, underscoring the Jester archetype's ability to provoke thought and inspire transformation.

Elegua and the Village Feast
In another story, Elegua visited a village that was preparing for a grand feast to honor the orisha. The villagers, eager to impress the orisha with their offerings, spared no effort in preparing an elaborate celebration. However, Elegua, known for his unpredictable nature, decided to test the villagers' sincerity.

Elegua arrived at the village disguised as a hungry wanderer and approached the villagers, asking for a small portion of food. The villagers, focused on their preparations, dismissed the wanderer, believing that their grand feast was more important than tending to a single beggar.

Later, as the feast commenced, Elegua revealed his true identity and pointed out the villagers' lack of generosity and compassion. The feast, despite its grandeur, had failed to honor the true spirit of giving and community. Elegua's lesson was clear: true devotion and honor come from acts of kindness and empathy, not just from elaborate displays.

This story reflects Elegua's role as a moral guide, using his trickster ways to reveal the importance of humility, generosity, and genuine compassion. Elegua's actions remind us that appearances can be deceiving and that the essence of any offering lies in its sincerity and intent.

Through these stories, Elegua demonstrates the multifaceted nature of the Jester archetype, using humor, wit, and trickery to impart valuable lessons. His narratives challenge individuals to reflect on their perspectives, question societal norms, and embrace the complexities of life with curiosity and resilience. Elegua's role as a trickster and teacher underscores the power of humor and playfulness as tools for transformation and growth, inviting us to explore the deeper truths that lie beneath the surface of our everyday experiences.

EXERCISES & RITUALS

Here are some exercises and rituals that can help individuals align with Elegua and the Jester archetype, emphasizing the importance of embracing one's inner child, humor, and laughter in a safe and responsible way. These activities are designed to channel the Jester's energies positively and productively, fostering creativity, connection, and joy.

Laughter Therapy Group Session

Supplies Needed:
- Comfortable seating (chairs or cushions)
- A space large enough to accommodate group activities
- A selection of humorous props (funny hats, wigs, etc.)
- Laughter-inducing videos or clips (optional)
- Music player with upbeat and lively music

Session Outline:

1. Welcome and Introduction (10 minutes)

    - Opening Circle: Gather participants in a circle and offer a warm welcome. Introduce the purpose of the session: to explore the healing power of laughter and to embrace the playful, joyful energy of the Jester archetype.

    - Icebreaker Activity: Begin with a quick icebreaker, such as having each participant share their name and a funny or embarrassing story.

This activity helps to create a relaxed and open atmosphere, breaking the ice and encouraging laughter from the start.

2. Laughter Warm-Up (10 minutes)

- Breathing Exercises: Lead the group in deep breathing exercises to relax and center themselves. Inhale deeply, hold for a few seconds, and exhale slowly, releasing any tension.

- Facial Warm-Up: Guide participants through a series of facial stretches and movements, such as exaggerated smiles, frowns, and wide-eyed expressions, to loosen facial muscles and prepare for laughter.

3. Structured Laughter Exercises (20 minutes)

- Simulated Laughter: Begin with simple exercises that encourage fake laughter. For example, have the group start with a low giggle and gradually increase in intensity to full belly laughs. Encourage participants to make eye contact, as laughter is contagious and can spread through the group.

- Laughter Games: Engage the group in a series of laughter games, such as:

- Laughing Circle: Have participants sit in a circle and pass a "laughter ball" around. Each person must catch the ball, laugh for a few seconds, and pass it on. The aim is to keep the laughter going and spread it around the group.

- Laughing Yoga: Lead the group in yoga-inspired poses that incorporate laughter, such as "Lion Laugh" (roaring with laughter like a lion) or "Laughing Cat" (moving through cat-cow poses with laughter).

- Laughter Meditation: Guide participants in a brief laughter meditation, where they close their eyes, focus on their breathing, and allow natural laughter to arise. Encourage participants to let go of any inhibitions and fully embrace the joy of laughter.

4. Creative Laughter Activities (20 minutes)

- Prop Play: Distribute humorous props like funny hats, wigs, or glasses. Encourage participants to put on the props and improvise short skits or funny scenarios. The aim is to encourage creativity and spontaneous laughter.

- Laughter Improv: Organize a short improv session where participants act out silly or absurd scenes suggested by the group. Allow for creativity and humor to flow freely, emphasizing fun over performance.

5. Group Reflection and Sharing (10 minutes)

- Closing Circle: Gather the group in a circle for a closing reflection. Invite participants to share their experiences and insights from the session. Encourage them to discuss how laughter and humor have impacted their mood, energy, and perspective.

- Gratitude Expression: Encourage participants to express gratitude for the shared experience, reinforcing the importance of community and connection.

6. Closing Ritual (10 minutes)

- Affirmations: Lead the group in a series of positive affirmations that emphasize joy, laughter, and well-being. Examples include "I embrace the joy of laughter in my life" or "I connect with others through humor and play."

- Parting Laughter: Conclude the session with a final group laugh, encouraging participants to carry the energy of laughter with them as they go about their day.

Explanation:
This laughter therapy group session provides a safe and inclusive space for participants to explore the healing power of humor and laughter. By embracing the Jester archetype, individuals can enhance their well-being, foster social connections, and cultivate a joyful and resilient outlook on life. Laughter therapy encourages the release of stress, boosts mood, and strengthens bonds within the community, making it a powerful tool for personal and collective transformation.

Comedy Sketch Creation and Performance

Supplies Needed:
- Notebooks and pens
- A selection of humorous props and costumes (hats, wigs, glasses, etc.)
- Optional: A small stage or designated performance area
- Music player with upbeat background music

Session Outline:

1. Welcome and Introduction (10 minutes)

    - Opening Circle: Begin the session by gathering participants in a circle. Welcome everyone and explain the purpose of the session: to create and perform comedy sketches that explore the power of humor and creativity.

- Icebreaker Activity: Start with a light-hearted icebreaker, such as having participants share a funny joke or an interesting fact about themselves. This activity helps build rapport and encourages a playful atmosphere.

2. Group Brainstorming and Sketch Creation (30 minutes)

- Form Teams: Divide participants into small groups of 3-5 people, ensuring a mix of personalities and creativity levels in each group.

- Brainstorming Session: Encourage each group to brainstorm ideas for a short comedy sketch. Provide prompts if needed, such as:

    - "An alien visiting Earth for the first time."
    - "A day in the life of a superhero with a quirky power."
    - "A hilariously dysfunctional family dinner."

- Script Writing: Give each group time to outline their sketch, focusing on key scenes, dialogue, and comedic elements. Encourage creativity and collaboration, emphasizing that the goal is to have fun and explore humor.

3. Prop Selection and Rehearsal (20 minutes)

- Select Props and Costumes: Allow groups to choose props and costumes from the selection provided. Encourage them to use these items creatively to enhance their sketches.

- Rehearsal Time: Give each group time to rehearse their sketch, experimenting with timing, delivery, and comedic elements. Encourage groups to support and provide feedback to one another, fostering a collaborative environment.

4. Performance and Laughter (30 minutes)

- Performance Setup: Designate an area for performances, such as a small stage or open space. Ensure that the audience is seated comfortably and can see the performers clearly.

- Group Performances: Invite each group to perform their comedy sketch in front of the other participants. Encourage the audience to engage, laugh, and applaud, creating a supportive and lively atmosphere.

- Feedback and Laughter: After each performance, allow time for feedback and laughter. Encourage participants to share what they enjoyed about the sketch and to highlight memorable moments.

5. Reflection and Sharing (10 minutes)

- Group Reflection: Gather participants for a closing reflection session. Invite them to share their thoughts on the creative process and their experiences during the performances.

- Discuss Insights: Facilitate a discussion about the role of humor and creativity in fostering connection and well-being. Encourage participants to reflect on how laughter and play can be integrated into their daily lives.

6. Closing Ritual (10 minutes)

- Gratitude Circle: Conclude the session with a gratitude circle, where participants express appreciation for each other's creativity, humor, and participation.

- Laughter Affirmations: Lead the group in laughter-focused affirmations, reinforcing the positive energy and joy experienced during the session. Examples include "I embrace creativity and laughter in my life" and "I am grateful for the joy and connections shared today."

Explanation:
This comedy sketch creation and performance activity allows participants to explore their creativity and humor in a supportive group setting. By engaging in collaborative creation and performance, individuals can strengthen their connections with others, build confidence, and experience the transformative power of laughter. This session aligns with the Jester archetype's emphasis on play, innovation, and joy, providing participants with a memorable and uplifting experience that enhances their well-being and sense of community.

Improvisation and Role-Play Games

Supplies Needed:
- Props or costumes (optional)
- Open space for movement

Guidelines:
1. Create a Safe Space: Choose a venue where participants feel comfortable expressing themselves. Encourage a playful and non-judgmental environment.

2. Warm-Up Exercises: Begin with warm-up activities, such as simple movement games or vocal exercises, to help participants loosen up and feel more comfortable.
3. Engage in Improvisation: Organize improvisation games that encourage spontaneity and creativity. Examples include:

   - Yes, And...: Players build on each other's ideas, promoting collaboration and active listening.
   - Character Creation: Participants create and embody a character, exploring different personas and scenarios.
   - Role-Playing Scenarios: Engage in role-play situations that allow participants to explore various perspectives and emotions.

4. Debrief and Reflect: After the games, gather participants to discuss their experiences. Reflect on the emotions and insights gained, emphasizing the value of humor and adaptability in everyday life.

Explanation:
Improvisation and role-play activities encourage participants to explore creativity and adaptability, key aspects of the Jester archetype. By embracing spontaneity and humor, individuals can develop greater resilience and resourcefulness, enhancing their ability to navigate life's challenges with a positive and open-minded approach.

Jester's Journey Storytelling Session

Supplies Needed:
- Storybooks or mythological texts
- Journal or notebook
- Pen

Guidelines:
1. Select Stories: Choose a collection of stories or myths that feature Jester-like characters or themes of humor and play. Consider works from various cultures and traditions.
2. Create a Storytelling Atmosphere: Set up a comfortable space for storytelling, using cushions, blankets, or soft lighting to create an inviting environment. Encourage participants to relax and engage with the stories.
3. Read or Listen to Stories: Share the selected stories with the group, encouraging active listening and engagement. Focus on themes of humor, creativity, and resilience as they relate to the Jester archetype.
4. Reflect and Discuss: After each story, facilitate a discussion about the themes and lessons presented. Encourage participants to draw parallels between the stories and their own experiences, exploring how the Jester archetype manifests in their lives.
5. Personal Storytelling: Invite participants to share personal anecdotes or experiences that resonate with the Jester archetype. Encourage creativity and humor, fostering a sense of community and connection.

Explanation:
Storytelling sessions provide a platform for exploring the Jester archetype through narratives and personal experiences. By engaging with stories of humor and transformation, individuals can gain insights into the Jester's role in their lives, cultivating a deeper understanding of its positive and empowering aspects.

These exercises and rituals offer various ways to connect with Elegua and the Jester archetype, encouraging individuals to embrace humor, playfulness, and creativity in their daily lives. By aligning with these energies, participants can enhance their well-being and resilience, fostering a more joyful and fulfilling existence.

THE JESTER

REFLECTIONS

The exploration of Elegua as the embodiment of the Jester archetype reveals a profound connection between humor, play, and wisdom. Through the tales and characteristics of Elegua, we see how laughter and mischief serve as powerful tools for transformation, inviting us to challenge our perceptions and embrace the unexpected. The Jester archetype, as personified by Elegua, reminds us of the importance of maintaining a light-hearted perspective, especially when faced with life's uncertainties and challenges.

Elegua's stories teach us that humor is not merely an escape from reality, but a lens through which we can gain deeper insight into the human experience. His playful antics and cunning nature serve as reminders of the need to balance levity with responsibility, urging us to approach life with a sense of curiosity and openness. By engaging with the Jester archetype, we are encouraged to explore the boundaries of our comfort zones, to question societal norms, and to find joy in the simple moments of life.

Moreover, the rituals and exercises associated with Elegua and the Jester archetype provide valuable opportunities for personal growth and self-discovery. Through activities such as laughter therapy, creative expression, and playful improvisation, individuals can cultivate a deeper connection with their inner child, fostering resilience and adaptability in the face of adversity. These practices highlight the transformative power of humor, offering a pathway to healing and empowerment that transcends cultural and individual differences.

Ultimately, the journey with Elegua and the Jester archetype invites us to embrace the beauty of imperfection and the magic of spontaneity. By integrating the qualities of playfulness, creativity, and joy into our lives, we can navigate the complexities of existence with grace and optimism, leaving a legacy of laughter and love for future generations.

Chapter 12

The Sage

The Sage archetype is characterized by wisdom, knowledge, and a deep-seated pursuit of truth. Sages are often seen as wise counselors and advisors, offering insight and guidance to those seeking understanding. They are typically associated with qualities such as intelligence, clarity of thought, and a profound curiosity about the mysteries of life. The Sage is driven by a desire to uncover the truths of the universe, seeking knowledge not only for its own sake but also to share it with others.

A hallmark trait of the Sage is their ability to see beyond the surface, to delve into the complexities and nuances of any situation. They possess an analytical mind and a keen awareness that allows them to discern patterns and connections that others might overlook. This depth of understanding makes them valuable sources of wisdom, capable of illuminating the paths forward in times of uncertainty.

The Sage's quest for knowledge often leads them to explore diverse fields, from philosophy and science to spirituality and the arts. They are lifelong learners who continuously seek to expand their horizons and deepen their understanding of the world. This insatiable curiosity fuels their growth and evolution, allowing them to offer profound insights and guidance to those around them.

Strengths and Weaknesses
The strengths of the Sage archetype lie in their intellectual prowess and ability to provide clarity and guidance. Sages are adept at analyzing complex situations and offering solutions based on logic and reason. Their insights can illuminate the way forward, helping others navigate challenges and make informed decisions. The Sage's wisdom is often sought in times of crisis, as they possess the ability to remain calm and centered, offering a steadying presence amidst chaos.

Moreover, the Sage's dedication to truth-seeking and knowledge acquisition enables them to challenge conventional thinking and push the boundaries of understanding. They are not afraid to question established beliefs and explore new ideas, making them catalysts for innovation and change. This willingness to explore uncharted territories can lead to breakthroughs and advancements that benefit society as a whole.

However, the Sage's strengths can also manifest as weaknesses if not balanced with emotional awareness and connection. The Sage's pursuit of knowledge can sometimes lead to detachment and isolation, as they may prioritize intellectual pursuits over interpersonal relationships. This detachment can result in a lack of empathy or understanding of the emotional needs of others, creating barriers to connection and collaboration.

Additionally, the Sage's focus on logic and reason can lead to a dismissal of intuitive or emotional insights, limiting their ability to fully comprehend the human experience. To overcome these challenges, Sages must learn to balance their intellectual pursuits with emotional intelligence, fostering a holistic approach to understanding and guidance.

THE SAGE

Cultural Examples

The Sage archetype is prevalent in literature, film, and mythology, often depicted as wise mentors, guides, and philosophers. These characters embody the quest for knowledge and truth, offering insights and wisdom to those they encounter.

One of the most iconic examples of the Sage archetype in literature is Gandalf from J.R.R. Tolkien's *The Lord of the Rings*. Gandalf is portrayed as a wise and powerful wizard who guides and mentors the story's protagonists. His deep knowledge of the world and its history allows him to provide crucial insights and counsel, aiding in the fight against darkness. Gandalf's role as a guide and protector highlights the Sage's ability to illuminate the path forward, offering wisdom and clarity in times of uncertainty.

In film, the character of Yoda from the *Star Wars* saga epitomizes the Sage archetype. As a wise and ancient Jedi Master, Yoda possesses immense knowledge and understanding of the Force. He serves as a mentor to young Jedi, imparting lessons about balance, patience, and the nature of power. Yoda's teachings emphasize the importance of inner wisdom and self-awareness, reflecting the Sage's commitment to guiding others on their journey toward enlightenment.

In mythology, the figure of Athena, the Greek goddess of wisdom and warfare, exemplifies the Sage archetype. Athena is revered for her intelligence, strategic thinking, and wise counsel. She is often depicted as a guiding force, offering protection and guidance to heroes in their quests. Athena's embodiment of wisdom and truth-seeking highlights the Sage's role as a source of guidance and illumination.

The Sage archetype also remains a force in contemporary society, particularly in the realms of education, philosophy, and intellectual pursuits. This archetype is embodied by figures who seek wisdom, knowledge, and truth, often serving as mentors or thought leaders. In the modern world, the Sage archetype is evident in the work of public intellectuals, such as Noam Chomsky or Yuval Noah Harari, who challenge conventional thinking and offer new insights into the complexities of human existence.

Historical or Contemporary Figures
Socrates (c. 470–399 BCE)
Socrates, the classical Greek philosopher, epitomizes the Sage archetype with his relentless pursuit of wisdom and truth. Socrates is best known for his method of questioning (the Socratic method), which encourages critical thinking and self-reflection. His dedication to seeking knowledge and challenging conventional wisdom, even at the cost of his life, marks him as a profound embodiment of the Sage.

Confucius (551–479 BCE)
Confucius, the Chinese philosopher and teacher, is another powerful example of the Sage archetype. His teachings on morality, ethics, and social harmony have deeply influenced Chinese culture and thought. Confucius's emphasis on wisdom, self-cultivation, and the importance of knowledge reflects the Sage's quest for understanding and enlightenment.

In Psychology
The Sage archetype is also relevant in the field of psychology, where it represents the pursuit of self-knowledge and personal growth. Jungian therapy, in particular, emphasizes the importance of integrating the Sage archetype as part of the individuation process, helping individuals to develop a deeper understanding of themselves and the world around them. The rise of mindfulness practices and the growing interest in ancient wisdom traditions, such as Buddhism and Stoicism, also reflect the Sage archetype's influence in modern life. These practices encourage individuals to cultivate wisdom, clarity, and inner peace, aligning with the Sage's timeless quest for truth and understanding.

Shadow Side

The shadow side of the Sage archetype emerges when the pursuit of knowledge and truth becomes detached from emotional awareness and empathy. Sages may become overly focused on intellectual pursuits, neglecting the importance of human connection and emotional understanding. This detachment can lead to isolation and a lack of meaningful relationships, as the Sage may prioritize knowledge over interpersonal connections.

The Sage's emphasis on logic and reason can also result in a dismissal of intuitive or emotional insights, limiting their ability to fully comprehend the complexities of the human experience. This rigid adherence to rationality can create barriers to understanding, as the Sage may struggle to connect with others on an emotional level or to appreciate the value of subjective experiences.

Moreover, the Sage's quest for truth can sometimes lead to arrogance or a sense of superiority, as they may perceive themselves as possessing greater knowledge or insight than others. This arrogance can create divisions and hinder collaboration, as the Sage may struggle to acknowledge the contributions and perspectives of others.

To navigate the shadow side of the Sage archetype, individuals must cultivate emotional intelligence and empathy, recognizing the importance of balancing intellect with compassion. By embracing the value of human connection and emotional awareness, Sages can transcend the limitations of their archetype and offer guidance that is both insightful and compassionate.

Path to Individuation

The path to individuation for the Sage archetype involves integrating intellectual pursuits with emotional intelligence and human connection. Sages must learn to balance their quest for knowledge with an awareness of the emotional and relational aspects of life, fostering a holistic approach to understanding and guidance.

One aspect of the individuation process for Sages is the development of emotional intelligence, which involves recognizing and understanding one's own emotions and the emotions of others. By cultivating empathy and compassion, Sages can enhance their ability to connect with others and to offer guidance that is both insightful and supportive.

Sages must also embrace the value of intuition and subjective experiences, recognizing that wisdom is not solely derived from logic and reason. By integrating intuitive insights with intellectual understanding, Sages can gain a deeper and more comprehensive perspective on the complexities of the human experience.

Additionally, Sages must learn to value collaboration and the contributions of others, recognizing that wisdom and knowledge are enriched by diverse perspectives. By fostering a sense of humility and openness, Sages can transcend the limitations of their archetype and contribute to collective growth and understanding.

Through the process of individuation, Sages can align their intellectual pursuits with their emotional and relational capacities, achieving a state of balance and harmony. This integration allows them to offer guidance and wisdom that is both insightful and compassionate, fostering a deeper understanding of the world and the human experience.

ORUNMILA AS THE SAGE

Orunmila, one of the principal deities in Yoruba mythology, epitomizes the Sage archetype through his association with wisdom, knowledge, and divination. Revered as the orisha of wisdom and prophecy, Orunmila is known for his deep understanding of the universe and his ability to guide individuals on their spiritual journeys.

Connection to the Sage Archetype
Orunmila's role as the guardian of knowledge and truth aligns him closely with the Sage archetype. He is often depicted as a wise elder, possessing profound insights into the mysteries of life and the cosmos. Orunmila's wisdom is sought in matters of destiny and fate, as he provides guidance and clarity through the practice of Ifa divination.

Orunmila's deep connection to the divine and his ability to access hidden knowledge make him a powerful guide and counselor. His teachings emphasize the importance of self-awareness, balance, and alignment with one's destiny. Orunmila's role as a spiritual advisor reflects the Sage's commitment to truth-seeking and the dissemination of wisdom.

Strengths and Weaknesses
Orunmila's strengths as the Sage archetype are evident in his ability to offer profound insights and guidance. His wisdom and clarity provide individuals with the tools to navigate the complexities of life and to make informed decisions. Orunmila's role as a mediator between the divine and the human realms underscores his significance as a source of guidance and enlightenment.

However, Orunmila's pursuit of knowledge can sometimes lead to detachment from the emotional aspects of life. His focus on intellectual understanding may result in a lack of empathy or connection with the human experience. To overcome these challenges, Orunmila must integrate his wisdom with compassion and emotional awareness, offering guidance that is both insightful and empathetic.

Cultural Significance

Orunmila holds a central place in Yoruba religion and its diasporic adaptations, serving as the custodian of Ifa, the divinatory system that provides guidance and insight. His teachings and practices are integral to the spiritual lives of practitioners, offering a pathway to understanding and alignment with one's destiny.

In addition to his religious significance, Orunmila is a symbol of resilience and adaptability. His ability to access and interpret divine knowledge reflects the Sage's role as a catalyst for transformation and growth. Orunmila's narratives offer valuable lessons on the power of wisdom and the importance of embracing the complexities of life.

Shadow Side

The shadow side of Orunmila's story is reflected in his potential for detachment and isolation. While Orunmila's wisdom is vast, his focus on intellectual pursuits can lead to a disconnect from the emotional and relational aspects of life. This detachment can create barriers to connection and understanding, limiting his ability to offer holistic guidance.

Orunmila's journey highlights the potential for wisdom to become rigid or dogmatic, as he may prioritize knowledge over intuitive or emotional insights. To navigate the shadow side of the Sage archetype, Orunmila must cultivate emotional intelligence and empathy, recognizing the importance of balancing intellect with compassion.

Path to Individuation

Orunmila's path to individuation involves integrating his profound wisdom with emotional awareness and human connection. By embracing his role as a guide and protector, Orunmila can channel his energy in ways that uplift and inspire others. His journey highlights the importance of balance, self-awareness, and meaningful connections, allowing him to transcend the limitations of the Sage archetype.

THE SAGE

Through his narratives, Orunmila teaches the value of wisdom and understanding while emphasizing the need for empathy and compassion. By aligning with the Sage archetype with intention and awareness, individuals can cultivate a life of insight, growth, and transformation.

ORUNMILA STORIES

Orunmila, the esteemed orisha of wisdom and divination in Yoruba mythology, is central to many stories that emphasize his role as a guide and protector of humanity. His narratives highlight his profound knowledge and his unique relationship with destiny and fate, demonstrating his integral role in the spiritual lives of the Yoruba people.

Orunmila and the Creation of the Universe
One of the foundational stories about Orunmila tells of his presence at the creation of the universe by Olodumare, the supreme deity in Yoruba cosmology. It is said that Orunmila witnessed the formation of the cosmos and the unfolding of the divine plan, granting him unparalleled insight into the workings of the universe. This knowledge bestowed upon him the ability to understand each person's destiny and path in life.

As a witness to creation, Orunmila became the custodian of the secrets of existence, making him a pivotal figure in the practice of Ifa divination. His presence at the creation ensures that he possesses a comprehensive understanding of the interconnectedness of all things, allowing him to guide individuals on their journeys and help them align with their destinies. This story underscores Orunmila's role as a sage and a seer, embodying the Sage archetype's pursuit of knowledge and truth.

The Curse of Opele
Another significant story involves Orunmila and his servant, Opele. Opele, known for his insolence and lack of respect, incurred Orunmila's wrath

through his continuous misbehavior. In response to Opele's actions, Orunmila decided to teach him a lesson by transforming him into a divination tool. This transformation turned Opele into a chain of seed pods, which Orunmila used in his divinatory practices.

The Opele divination chain became an essential tool for Orunmila, allowing him to communicate with the spiritual realm and gain insights into the future. This story highlights Orunmila's wisdom and creativity, as he transformed a negative situation into a powerful asset. It also reflects the Sage archetype's ability to find solutions and create positive outcomes from adversity.

The tale of Opele serves as a reminder of the consequences of disrespect and the importance of humility and reverence in spiritual matters. Orunmila's actions demonstrate his commitment to justice and the maintenance of harmony within the spiritual realm.

Orunmila and Iku (Death)
A compelling narrative involving Orunmila features his encounter with Iku, the personification of Death. During a time when Iku was rampant and indiscriminately taking lives, Orunmila stepped forward to challenge her. Recognizing the need to restore balance, Orunmila engaged in a battle with Iku to curb her unchecked power.

Through his wisdom and strategic thinking, Orunmila was able to defeat Iku in battle, securing an agreement that would spare those who wore a green and yellow-beaded bracelet from an untimely death. This agreement symbolized Orunmila's ability to mediate between the forces of life and death, emphasizing his role as a protector and guide for humanity.

This story reflects the Sage archetype's strength in negotiating and harmonizing opposing forces, illustrating Orunmila's profound understanding of the delicate balance between life and death. His victory over Iku underscores his commitment to preserving life and supporting individuals on their spiritual paths.

These stories of Orunmila reveal his deep connection to the mysteries of the universe and his unwavering dedication to guiding and protecting humanity. As the embodiment of the Sage archetype, Orunmila's wisdom and insight continue to inspire and inform the spiritual practices of the Yoruba people and their descendants. His narratives offer timeless lessons on the importance of knowledge, balance, and understanding in navigating the complexities of life, demonstrating the enduring relevance and power of the Sage archetype.

EXERCISES & RITUALS

Here are some exercises and rituals designed to help individuals align with Orunmila and the Sage archetype. These activities focus on balancing intellect with compassion, avoiding rigidity or dogmatism, and preventing detachment or social isolation.

Coin Divination for Insight and Wisdom

Supplies Needed:
- Three coins (any denomination)
- A small cloth or mat for casting
- A journal or notebook
- A pen or pencil
- A quiet space free from distractions

Disclaimer: This exercise is not a traditional Yoruba or Lukumi practice and is only intended for personal reflection and insight. It is suitable for anyone to perform, regardless of their level of initiation.

Guidelines:

1. Prepare the Space

    - Select a quiet and comfortable space where you can focus without interruptions. Lay out a cloth or mat on which to cast the coins. This helps create a defined area for the divination and adds a sense of ritual to the process.

2. Set Your Intention

    - Take a moment to center yourself and set a clear intention for the divination session. Think about a specific question or area of your life where you seek guidance. Your question should be open-ended and reflective, inviting insight rather than a simple yes or no answer. Examples of questions might include:

        - "What wisdom do I need to embrace at this moment in my life?"
        - "How can I better balance my intellectual pursuits with emotional awareness?"
        - "What should I focus on to achieve personal growth and transformation?"

3. Prepare the Coins

    - Hold the three coins in your hands and focus on your intention. Ask for guidance and clarity. Take a few deep breaths to calm your mind and attune yourself to the energy of the divination.

4. Cast the Coins

    - When you feel ready, gently cast the coins onto the cloth or mat. Observe how they land, noting whether each coin shows heads or tails. This combination of heads and tails will provide the basis for your reading.

5. Interpreting the Results

    - Use the pattern of heads and tails to interpret the reading. Each combination can have different meanings, providing insight into your question or situation.

    - Possible Interpretations:

        - **Three Heads:** Represents clarity, alignment, and a strong affirmative answer. This may indicate that you are on the right path and should trust your intuition and insights.
        - **Two Heads, One Tail:** Suggests a need for balance and consideration. You may need to weigh different perspectives or options before making a decision.
        - **Two Tails, One Head:** Indicates challenges or obstacles that require attention. Reflect on potential issues and consider strategies to overcome them.
        - **Three Tails:** Symbolizes caution or a need for reevaluation. This result may suggest rethinking your current path or approach and considering alternative solutions.

6. Reflect and Journal

    - After interpreting the results, spend some time reflecting on the insights gained from the reading. Write down your observations and thoughts in a journal. Consider how these insights apply to your question and how you might incorporate them into your life. Journaling helps deepen your understanding and solidifies the wisdom gained from the divination process.

7. Conclude the Session

    - Conclude the session by expressing gratitude for the guidance received. Gather the coins and return them to their container, and take a few moments to ground yourself with deep breaths.

Explanation:
This simple coin divination exercise offers a practical and accessible way to facilitate insight and wisdom through a reflective process. By engaging in this form of cleromancy, individuals can explore their inner thoughts and emotions, balance intellect with intuition, and gain valuable guidance for personal growth. This practice encourages a holistic approach to decision-making and self-discovery, empowering individuals to navigate their life's path with clarity and understanding.

Shared Wisdom Gathering

Supplies Needed:
- Comfortable seating arranged in a circle
- A central item (such as a candle or a talking stick) to signify the speaker's turn
- A selection of wisdom-based books or personal objects related to the stories being shared (optional)
- Notebook and pen for each participant for reflection

Guidelines:

1. Create the Environment

- Set up the space with chairs or cushions arranged in a circle to promote open communication and equality among participants. Place a symbolic object, such as a candle or talking stick, in the center of the circle. This object will be passed around to indicate whose turn it is to speak.

2. Opening Reflection

    - Begin with a moment of silence to center the group and set the intention for the gathering. Encourage participants to reflect on the themes of wisdom and connection. Invite each participant to silently consider a piece of wisdom or a life lesson they would like to share with the group.

3. Sharing Wisdom

    - Encourage participants to take turns sharing a personal story, cultural myth, or piece of wisdom that has been meaningful in their lives. Participants can draw inspiration from a favorite book, cultural narrative, or personal experience. The person holding the talking stick has the floor, ensuring everyone has the opportunity to speak without interruption. Encourage them to speak from the heart, offering their insights and reflections openly.

4. Facilitate Discussion

    - After each story, open the floor for discussion. Invite participants to share their thoughts, reflections, and any lessons they've drawn from the story. Ask questions like:

        - "What resonated with you about this story?"
        - "How can the wisdom shared be applied in our lives?"

- ▪ "What new perspectives or insights did you gain from this story?"

  - This discussion phase allows participants to delve deeper into the wisdom presented and to explore its relevance to their own lives.

5. Reflective Journaling

   - Provide time for participants to write in their journals, reflecting on the stories and insights shared during the gathering. Encourage them to consider how they can incorporate the wisdom into their daily lives and personal growth journey.

6. Closing Ritual

   - End the session with a collective affirmation or moment of gratitude. Each participant can share one piece of wisdom they will carry forward, reinforcing the lessons learned and the connections made during the gathering.

Explanation:
The Shared Wisdom Gathering combines storytelling and discussion to create a rich tapestry of insights and experiences. By sharing and reflecting on stories, participants connect with the Sage archetype, exploring the depths of wisdom and empathy. This exercise encourages the balance of intellect and compassion, fostering a supportive community where diverse perspectives are valued. Through this shared experience, individuals can cultivate a deeper understanding of themselves and others, promoting personal growth and social connection.

Mindfulness and Compassion Retreat

Supplies Needed:
- A quiet, serene location (such as a retreat center or natural setting)
- Meditation cushions or mats
- Journals and pens

Guidelines:
1. Retreat Setup: Organize a day-long retreat in a peaceful location. Prepare activities that combine mindfulness practices with discussions on compassion and empathy.
2. Morning Meditation: Begin with a guided meditation session focused on cultivating awareness and presence. Encourage participants to observe their thoughts and emotions without judgment.
3. Compassion Workshop: Lead a workshop on the importance of compassion and empathy. Include exercises that encourage participants to practice self-compassion and extend kindness to others.
4. Silent Reflection: Allocate time for silent reflection, where participants can journal their thoughts and insights. Encourage them to consider how they can integrate mindfulness and compassion into their daily lives.
5. Group Sharing and Closing: End the retreat with a group sharing session, allowing participants to express what they've learned and how they plan to apply it.

Explanation:
A mindfulness and compassion retreat provides an immersive experience that helps individuals align with the Sage archetype by fostering a balanced approach to self-awareness, empathy, and intellectual growth.

Creative Problem-Solving Workshop

Supplies Needed:
- Flip charts or whiteboards
- Markers and sticky notes
- A set of complex, open-ended problems or scenarios

Guidelines:
1. Introduce the Workshop: Begin by explaining the goals of the workshop: to engage in creative problem-solving while balancing intellect with collaboration and empathy.
2. Present Scenarios: Provide participants with complex problems or scenarios that require innovative thinking and collaboration. Encourage them to approach these challenges with an open mind.
3. Group Brainstorming: Divide participants into small groups and facilitate a brainstorming session. Use tools like mind mapping or role-playing to explore different solutions and perspectives.
4. Evaluate Solutions: Have each group present their proposed solutions. Encourage constructive feedback and discussion, highlighting the importance of empathy and diverse perspectives in problem-solving.
5. Reflection: Conclude with a group reflection on the process. Discuss how the exercise helped balance intellect with emotional understanding and how these skills can be applied to real-life challenges.

Explanation:
This workshop emphasizes the Sage archetype's strength in problem-solving and innovation. By combining analytical thinking with empathy and collaboration, individuals can develop well-rounded solutions that address both intellectual and human aspects.

THE SAGE

These exercises and rituals offer various pathways to align with Orunmila and the Sage archetype, promoting a balanced approach to intellect, compassion, and personal growth. By engaging in these practices, individuals can cultivate wisdom and insight while fostering meaningful connections with themselves and others.

REFLECTIONS

Embracing the Sage archetype through the lens of Orunmila offers profound lessons in wisdom, balance, and insight. His stories and attributes illuminate the path to integrating knowledge with empathy, urging us to seek not only intellectual understanding but also compassionate engagement with the world around us. By reflecting on Orunmila's narratives and engaging in thoughtful practices, we can strive to balance our inner sage's wisdom with the heart's empathy, creating a more harmonious and enlightened approach to life.

Orunmila's legacy as a witness to creation, a guide in divination, and a mediator between life and death underscores the timeless relevance of the Sage archetype. His ability to transform challenges into opportunities for growth and his commitment to guiding humanity toward clarity and understanding provide a model for our own journeys. Through exercises like personal divination, reflective journaling, and mindful meditation, we can connect with our inner wisdom and cultivate a deeper awareness of our paths.

The teachings of Orunmila remind us that true wisdom encompasses both the intellect and the heart. By honoring this balance, we can navigate life's complexities with grace and insight, fostering a sense of purpose and fulfillment. As we move forward, let us carry the lessons of Orunmila with us, embracing the Sage's quest for knowledge, truth, and compassionate understanding in every aspect of our lives.

Chapter 13

The Magician

The Magician archetype is a powerful figure of transformation, vision, and power. In Jungian psychology, the Magician is the wise and transformative force that has the ability to manipulate reality, channel energy, and bring about profound change. This archetype represents the potential for mastery over the elements and the capacity to transform oneself and the world through insight and knowledge. The Magician's realm is one of possibilities, imagination, and the bridging of the physical and spiritual worlds. In this chapter, we explore the Magician archetype through the lens of Osanyin, the orisha of herbal medicine and healing, whose profound mastery of nature and transformative abilities make him an embodiment of this archetype.

Characteristics and Traits

The Magician archetype is characterized by transformation, vision, and power. This archetype represents the ability to see beyond the ordinary and transform reality through insight and action. Magicians are visionary figures, often depicted as wise and enigmatic, who can harness the forces of the universe to bring about change. They possess a deep understanding of the natural and supernatural realms and have the power to alter perception and reality. This archetype embodies the potential for mastery over one's environment and the self, often using knowledge, wisdom, and skill to achieve desired outcomes.

In mythology and folklore, the Magician is often depicted as a mentor or guide who helps others realize their potential. This archetype is associated with alchemy, transformation, and the pursuit of hidden knowledge. The Magician's vision extends beyond the mundane, allowing them to see connections and possibilities that others might overlook. Their power lies not just in their ability to create change but in their capacity to inspire transformation in others, encouraging them to explore their own potential and embrace change as a natural part of life.

Strengths and Weaknesses
The Magician archetype embodies mastery and manipulation, highlighting the fine line between constructive transformation and potential misuse of power. One of the Magician's greatest strengths is their ability to see beyond the surface and understand the deeper workings of the world. This insight allows them to effect change and inspire others, using their vision to guide and transform. The Magician's mastery over their craft enables them to navigate complex situations and bring about positive change, often serving as a catalyst for growth and innovation.

However, the Magician's strengths can also become weaknesses if misused. The potential for manipulation and control can lead to arrogance and hubris, as the Magician may become too focused on their own power and abilities. This can result in a detachment from reality and an overreliance on their perceived mastery, leading to ethical dilemmas and unintended consequences. The challenge for the Magician is to balance their desire for transformation with humility and integrity, ensuring that their actions are guided by a sense of responsibility and compassion.

THE MAGICIAN

Cultural Examples

In literature, film, and mythology, the Magician archetype is represented by characters who embody the transformative power of knowledge and vision. Merlin from Arthurian legend is a classic example of the Magician, serving as a mentor and guide to King Arthur, using his magical abilities to shape the destiny of the kingdom. Merlin's wisdom and foresight make him a quintessential Magician, transforming both the world around him and the individuals he guides through his deep understanding of magic and strategy.

Another iconic representation of the Magician archetype is Professor Albus Dumbledore from J.K. Rowling's *Harry Potter* series. As the wise and powerful headmaster of Hogwarts School of Witchcraft and Wizardry, Dumbledore guides the protagonist, Harry Potter, through his journey of self-discovery and transformation. Dumbledore's deep knowledge of magic, combined with his ability to see beyond the surface and understand the deeper implications of events, allows him to orchestrate the fight against dark forces. His mentorship and strategic planning underscore his role as a visionary who balances power with compassion and insight, guiding others toward growth and change.

In film, Morpheus from *The Matrix* embodies the Magician archetype, serving as a guide to the protagonist, Neo, and helping him unlock his potential and transform reality. Morpheus's deep understanding of the world's true nature and his ability to manipulate perception highlight the Magician's capacity to see beyond the surface and inspire change. His character demonstrates the power of belief and the transformative potential of knowledge, as he empowers Neo to challenge the status quo and embrace his destiny.

These cultural examples highlight the Magician archetype's role as a catalyst for transformation and growth. By using their knowledge and vision to guide others, these characters exemplify the Magician's ability to inspire change and foster personal and collective evolution. Through their journeys, they remind us of the importance of wisdom, insight, and the power of transformation in navigating life's challenges and opportunities.

Historical or Contemporary Figures
Isaac Newton (1642–1727)
Sir Isaac Newton, the English mathematician, physicist, and alchemist, represents the Magician archetype through his groundbreaking discoveries and his deep engagement with the mysteries of the natural world. Newton's work in developing the laws of motion and universal gravitation transformed our understanding of the universe, exemplifying the Magician's role in harnessing knowledge and power for transformative purposes.

Marie Curie (1867–1934)
Marie Curie, the Polish-French physicist and chemist, is another embodiment of the Magician archetype. Curie's pioneering research on radioactivity, which earned her two Nobel Prizes, reflects the Magician's pursuit of knowledge and mastery over unseen forces. Her work not only advanced science but also brought about significant societal changes, particularly in the fields of medicine and physics.

In Psychology
The Magician archetype is also significant in modern psychology, particularly in practices that involve self-transformation and personal growth. Techniques such as visualization, hypnosis, and cognitive-behavioral therapy draw on the Magician archetype's energy to help individuals reframe their thoughts and behaviors, leading to profound changes in their lives. The rise of the wellness industry and the growing interest in holistic health practices also reflect the Magician's influence, as individuals seek to harness the mind-body connection to achieve greater well-being. The Magician archetype reminds us of the transformative power of knowledge, vision, and intentionality in shaping our lives and the world around us.

Shadow Side

The shadow side of the Magician archetype manifests in manipulation, deceit, and the misuse of power. When the Magician becomes consumed by their own abilities, they may use their knowledge and skills to control and manipulate others for personal gain. This can lead to ethical dilemmas and a detachment from reality, as the Magician becomes more focused on their own power than on the well-being of others.

The Magician's shadow side also includes the potential for arrogance and hubris, as they may believe they are above the laws of nature and morality. This can result in a sense of invincibility and a disregard for the consequences of their actions. The challenge for the Magician is to recognize the limits of their power and to use their abilities responsibly, ensuring that their actions are guided by compassion and integrity.

Path to Individuation

The path to individuation for the Magician archetype involves balancing mastery with humility and using one's abilities for the greater good. The Magician must learn to integrate their vision and power with a sense of responsibility and compassion, ensuring that their actions are guided by ethical principles and a desire to serve others. This involves recognizing the limits of their power and embracing the interconnectedness of all things, using their abilities to inspire and transform rather than control and manipulate.

To achieve individuation, the Magician must cultivate self-awareness and mindfulness, recognizing the potential for their strengths to become weaknesses. By embracing their shadow side and acknowledging the potential for misuse of power, the Magician can develop a more balanced and holistic approach to transformation and change. This involves embracing vulnerability and recognizing the importance of collaboration and connection, using their abilities to empower others and create positive change in the world.

OSANYIN AS THE MAGICIAN

Osanyin, the orisha of herbal medicine and healing, embodies the Magician archetype through his profound mastery of nature and transformative abilities. As the keeper of the secrets of plants and herbs, Osanyin holds the knowledge of healing and transformation, using his wisdom to guide and heal those in need. His connection to the natural world and his ability to harness the power of plants highlight his role as a transformative figure, embodying the essence of the Magician archetype.

Characteristics and Traits
Osanyin's role as the orisha of herbal medicine reflects the Magician's characteristics of transformation, vision, and power. His deep understanding of the healing properties of plants and herbs allows him to transform illness into health, using his knowledge to bring about change and renewal. Osanyin's connection to nature and his ability to harness its power make him a symbol of the Magician's transformative abilities, guiding individuals on their journey of healing and growth.

As the keeper of the secrets of nature, Osanyin embodies the Magician's vision and mastery, using his knowledge to inspire and guide others. His ability to see beyond the surface and understand the deeper workings of the natural world highlights his role as a wise and powerful figure, capable of bringing about transformation and change. Osanyin's presence as the Magician encourages individuals to embrace their own potential for transformation and to harness the power of nature in their journey of personal growth.

Strengths and Weaknesses
Osanyin's strengths lie in his mastery of herbal medicine and his ability to transform illness into health. His knowledge of the healing properties of plants and herbs enables him to guide and inspire others, using his abilities

to bring about positive change. Osanyin's role as a healer and guide reflects the Magician's capacity for transformation and renewal, using his vision and mastery to inspire and empower those around him.

However, Osanyin's strengths can also become weaknesses if misused. The potential for manipulation and control exists if his knowledge is used for personal gain or to exert power over others. The challenge for Osanyin is to balance his mastery with humility and integrity, ensuring that his actions are guided by a sense of responsibility and compassion. By embracing the limits of his power and using his abilities for the greater good, Osanyin can embody the Magician's transformative potential in a balanced and holistic way.

Cultural Examples
In Yoruba mythology, Osanyin is revered as the orisha of herbal medicine and healing, embodying the Magician archetype through his mastery of nature and transformation. His role as a healer and guide is reflected in various stories and rituals that highlight his connection to the natural world and his ability to harness its power for healing and growth. Osanyin's presence in cultural narratives and practices underscores his role as a transformative figure, guiding individuals on their journey of personal and spiritual growth.

Osanyin's embodiment of the Magician archetype is also reflected in his role as a teacher and mentor, guiding individuals in their exploration of the natural world and its healing properties. His wisdom and mastery of herbal medicine inspire others to embrace their own potential for transformation and to connect with the natural world in their journey of personal growth. Through his teachings and guidance, Osanyin embodies the Magician's vision and power, using his abilities to inspire and empower those around him.

Shadow Side

The shadow side of Osanyin as the Magician archetype manifests in the potential for manipulation and misuse of power. If his knowledge of herbal medicine is used for personal gain or to exert control over others, Osanyin's strengths can become weaknesses, leading to ethical dilemmas and unintended consequences. The challenge for Osanyin is to balance his mastery with humility and integrity, ensuring that his actions are guided by a sense of responsibility and compassion.

Osanyin's shadow side also includes the potential for arrogance and detachment, as his focus on mastery and transformation may lead to a disconnect from the emotional and relational aspects of healing. To overcome this shadow side, Osanyin must embrace the interconnectedness of all things and recognize the importance of collaboration and connection in his journey of personal growth. By integrating his shadow side and using his abilities for the greater good, Osanyin can embody the Magician's transformative potential in a balanced and holistic way.

Path to Individuation

The path to individuation for Osanyin as the Magician archetype involves balancing mastery with humility and using his abilities for the greater good. Osanyin must learn to integrate his vision and power with a sense of responsibility and compassion, ensuring that his actions are guided by ethical principles and a desire to serve others. This involves recognizing the limits of his power and embracing the interconnectedness of all things, using his abilities to inspire and transform rather than control and manipulate.

To achieve individuation, Osanyin must cultivate self-awareness and mindfulness, recognizing the potential for his strengths to become weaknesses. By embracing his shadow side and acknowledging the potential for misuse of power, Osanyin can develop a more balanced and holistic approach to transformation and change. This involves embracing vulnerability and recognizing the importance of collaboration and connection, using his abilities to empower others and create positive change in the world. By following this path, Osanyin can embody the Magician's transformative potential and inspire others to embrace their own journey of growth and transformation.

OSANYIN STORIES

Osanyin, the orisha of herbal medicine and healing, holds a prominent place within Yoruba mythology and spiritual practice. His mastery over the plant kingdom and his role as the keeper of herbal secrets make him a powerful figure associated with knowledge, transformation, and healing. Several stories about Osanyin highlight his unique attributes and his interactions with other orisha, underscoring his significance as a transformative force.

Osanyin and the Secrets of the Forest
One of the most well-known stories about Osanyin revolves around his possession of all the knowledge of plants and herbs, which he kept locked away within a magical calabash. According to the myth, Osanyin was so protective of this knowledge that he hid it deep within the forest, making it inaccessible to all but himself. The other orisha, recognizing the power and potential of Osanyin's knowledge, became envious and sought to access it. However, Osanyin was clever and cunning, ensuring that the secrets remained hidden from those who might misuse them.

In this story, it was Orunmila, the orisha of wisdom and divination, who decided to outwit Osanyin to gain access to the herbal secrets. He devised a plan and enlisted the help of a bird to fly above the calabash and knock it from the tree where it was hidden. As the calabash fell and shattered, the secrets of herbal medicine were released into the world, scattered across the land for all to access. This story underscores the importance of sharing knowledge and the transformative power of wisdom. Osanyin's reluctance to share his knowledge highlights his role as a guardian of sacred information, while Orunmila's intervention emphasizes the necessity of using knowledge for the greater good.

Osanyin's Alliance with the Trees

Another captivating story about Osanyin involves his unique relationship with the trees and the natural world. It is said that Osanyin was born with only one leg, arm, and eye, which made him less mobile and visually aware than other orisha. However, his perceived physical limitations did not hinder him; instead, they reinforced his deep connection with the natural environment. Osanyin's reliance on the trees for support and movement within the forest exemplifies his symbiotic relationship with nature.

The trees, recognizing Osanyin's reverence and respect for their power, pledged their loyalty to him, offering their branches and roots to aid him in his movements and endeavors. This alliance made Osanyin exceptionally powerful, as he could command the trees to do his bidding, utilizing their strength and stability to navigate the forest. This story highlights Osanyin's intimate relationship with nature and illustrates his embodiment of the Magician archetype. He transforms his perceived weaknesses into strengths by harnessing the power of the natural world.

Osanyin's Conflict with Oya

Osanyin's interactions with other orisha further highlight his complex nature and his embodiment of the Magician archetype. One notable story involves a conflict with Oya, the orisha of winds, storms, and transformation. Oya sought to learn the secrets of herbal medicine from Osanyin to aid her community, but he refused to share his knowledge, viewing it as his exclusive domain.

In response, Oya summoned a powerful storm to uproot the plants in Osanyin's forest, scattering them far and wide. This act symbolized the democratization of knowledge, making the healing properties of plants accessible to all. Despite Osanyin's initial resistance, this event forced him to acknowledge the necessity of sharing his wisdom for the benefit of the community. Oya's actions highlight her own transformative power and align with the Magician archetype's themes of change and innovation. This story underscores the balance between knowledge and accessibility and the importance of using wisdom for communal benefit.

Osanyin's Role as a Healer
Osanyin's reputation as a healer is further illustrated in stories that depict his ability to cure ailments and restore balance through his mastery of herbal medicine. In many tales, Osanyin is sought by individuals suffering from various afflictions, and he uses his profound understanding of plants to create remedies and cures. His healing abilities are not only a testament to his knowledge but also to his compassion and dedication to serving others.

One story tells of a village plagued by a mysterious illness that no other orisha could cure. The villagers turned to Osanyin, who, through careful observation and understanding of the symptoms, identified the plants needed to heal the community. His intervention saved the village and solidified his reputation as a powerful healer and a wise and benevolent orisha. This story illustrates the transformative power of knowledge and the critical role of the Magician archetype in fostering healing and change.

Osanyin's stories exemplify the qualities of the Magician archetype, emphasizing transformation, mastery, and the power of knowledge. Through his interactions with other orisha and his connection to the natural world, Osanyin demonstrates the transformative potential of wisdom and the importance of using knowledge for the greater good. These tales remind us of the delicate balance between power and responsibility and the need to harness our abilities to foster growth, healing, and positive change. By embodying the Magician archetype, Osanyin serves as an enduring symbol of the transformative power of knowledge and the potential for healing and renewal in the natural world.

EXERCISES & RITUALS

Creating an Herbal Talisman

<u>Supplies Needed</u>:
- Small, flat stones or wooden discs
- Paints or markers
- Dried herbs (rosemary, thyme, and bay leaves)
- Small pouches or fabric squares
- A piece of string or ribbon
- A journal

<u>Guidelines</u>:

1. Choosing and Preparing Your Materials

    - Select a small, flat stone or wooden disc as the base for your talisman. Gather dried herbs known for their protective and healing properties, such as rosemary (protection), thyme (courage), and bay leaves (strength). Have small pouches or fabric squares ready to hold the herbs.

2. Painting or Decorating the Talisman

    - Using paints or markers, decorate the stone or wooden disc with symbols or designs that resonate with your intention. You might choose symbols of protection, strength, or personal significance. As you decorate, focus on infusing the talisman with your energy and intention.

3. Assembling the Talisman

    - Once the talisman is decorated and dry, place it in the center of the small pouch or fabric square. Add a pinch of each dried herb to the pouch, visualizing their properties combining to support and protect you. Gather the edges of the fabric and tie it securely with a piece of string or ribbon, forming a small bundle.

4. Charging the Talisman

    - Hold the talisman in your hands and close your eyes. Focus on your intention and visualize the energy of Osanyin and the Magician archetype flowing into the talisman. Imagine the talisman glowing with a protective and transformative light. Speak your intention aloud, affirming the purpose of the talisman.

5. Using the Talisman

    - Carry the talisman with you, or place it in a significant location, such as under your pillow or near your workspace. Use the talisman as a focal point during meditation or moments when you need strength and protection. Reflect on your experiences in your journal, noting any insights or changes you observe.

Explanation:
Creating an herbal talisman is a powerful way to harness the protective and transformative energy of Osanyin and the Magician archetype. This exercise helps to focus your intention and channel positive energies towards your goals. By combining the properties of herbs with a personally crafted symbol, you create a tangible reminder of the changes you wish to manifest, helping to align your actions with your desired transformation.

Herbal Tea Ritual for Insight

Supplies Needed:
- Dried herbs (chamomile, peppermint, and lemon balm)
- A teapot and cup
- A strainer or tea infuser
- A quiet space
- A journal

Guidelines:

1. Preparing the Tea

    - Choose a blend of dried herbs known for their calming and clarifying properties. Chamomile promotes relaxation, peppermint stimulates the mind, and lemon balm soothes and balances emotions. Combine the herbs in a strainer or tea infuser and place them in the teapot.

2. Boiling the Water

    - Boil water and pour it over the herbs, allowing them to steep for several minutes. As the tea brews, focus on your intention for insight and clarity. Visualize the energy of Osanyin infusing the tea with wisdom and guidance.

3. Setting the Space

    - Find a quiet space where you can sit comfortably and reflect. Light a candle if desired, creating a peaceful and focused environment. Pour the brewed tea into a cup, holding it gently in your hands.

4. Drinking the Tea

    - As you drink the tea, take slow, mindful sips. Focus on the taste, temperature, and aroma, grounding yourself in the present moment. Allow the calming properties of the herbs to relax your mind and open you to insight and reflection.

5. Reflecting and Journaling

    - After finishing the tea, take a few moments to sit quietly and reflect. Pay attention to any thoughts, feelings, or insights that arise. Use your journal to document your reflections, exploring any new understandings or clarity you have gained.

Explanation:
An herbal tea ritual is a simple yet profound way to connect with the wisdom and insight of Osanyin and the Magician archetype. This exercise encourages mindfulness, relaxation, and reflection, helping to clear the mind and open it to new perspectives. By incorporating herbs known for their calming and clarifying properties, you create a nurturing space for personal growth and insight.

Planting a Healing Garden

Supplies Needed:
- Seeds or seedlings of healing herbs (e.g., basil, thyme, peppermint, and calendula)
- Gardening tools
- Pots or a garden bed
- A small watering can
- A journal

Guidelines:

1. Selecting Your Herbs

    - Choose a variety of healing herbs that resonate with you and your intentions. Consider herbs known for their medicinal properties, such as basil for clarity, thyme for courage, peppermint for energy, and calendula for healing.

2. Preparing the Soil

    - Find a suitable spot in your garden or use pots if you have limited space. Prepare the soil by loosening it and adding any necessary nutrients. As you work the soil, focus on your intention for the garden, infusing the earth with your energy and purpose.

3. Planting the Herbs

    - Plant the seeds or seedlings, giving each herb enough space to grow. As you place each one in the soil, speak your intentions aloud, asking for the herbs' guidance and support in your journey towards transformation and healing.

4. Nurturing the Garden

    - Water the herbs gently, ensuring they receive the right amount of sunlight and care. Visit your garden regularly, tending to the plants and observing their growth. Use this time to reflect on your own growth and transformation, connecting with the energy of Osanyin and the Magician archetype.

5. Harvesting and Using the Herbs

    - Once the herbs have grown, harvest them mindfully, giving thanks for their gifts. Use the herbs in teas, baths, or charms, incorporating their healing properties into your rituals and daily life. Keep a journal to document your experiences and the insights you gain from nurturing your healing garden.

Explanation:
Planting a healing garden is a practical and symbolic way to align with the transformative energy of Osanyin and the Magician archetype. This exercise encourages mindfulness, patience, and a deep connection with nature. By nurturing the garden and using the herbs in your rituals, you create a tangible link to the natural world and its healing properties, fostering personal growth and transformation.

Crafting a Wand for Transformation

Supplies Needed:
- A suitable branch or stick from a tree
- Sandpaper (various grits)
- Knife or carving tools (optional)
- Beeswax or wood polish
- Small crystals, stones, or decorations (optional)
- Glue (optional)
- Small cloth pouch or ribbon

Choosing Your Wood:

    - **Apple:** Known for love, healing, and immortality. Apple wood is ideal for those seeking to cultivate relationships and promote well-being.

- **Ash:** Represents transformation, protection, and prosperity. Ash is often used in wands for its adaptability and grounding energy.
- **Birch:** Known for renewal, purification, and new beginnings. Birch wood is excellent for those embarking on a new journey or seeking to cleanse their energy.
- **Cedar:** Associated with purification, protection, and healing. Cedar is ideal for those seeking to create a sacred space or promote spiritual well-being.
- **Cherry:** Symbolizes love, divination, and rejuvenation. Cherry wood is excellent for those seeking to enhance their romantic and intuitive energies.
- **Elder:** Represents healing, regeneration, and protection. Elder is a powerful wood for those looking to work on personal growth and recovery.
- **Hazel:** Known for wisdom, knowledge, and divination. Hazel wood is excellent for those seeking to enhance their intellectual and spiritual insights.
- **Holly:** Associated with protection, strength, and eternal life. Holly is often used in wands for its powerful protective qualities.
- **Mahogany:** Symbolizes strength, endurance, and leadership. Mahogany is ideal for those seeking to boost their confidence and take control of their lives.
- **Maple:** Symbolizes balance, promise, and practicality. Maple wood is ideal for those seeking to bring harmony and stability into their lives.
- **Oak:** Known for strength, protection, and endurance. Oak is often used in magical workings that require stability and resilience.
- **Peach:** Associated with love, wisdom, and longevity. Peach wood is excellent for those seeking to foster loving relationships and personal growth.

THE MAGICIAN

- **Pine:** Represents purification, healing, and vitality. Pine wood is excellent for those looking to boost their energy and promote overall well-being.
- **Rowan:** Associated with protection, power, and success. Rowan wood is ideal for those seeking to boost their confidence and achieve their goals.
- **Willow:** Associated with intuition, dreams, and emotional healing. Willow wood is ideal for those looking to enhance their psychic abilities and emotional balance.
- **Yew:** Symbolizes transformation, endurance, and eternal life. Yew wood is often used in wands for its powerful connection to the cycles of life and death.

Guidelines:

1. Choosing the Right Branch

    - Find a branch or stick from one of the trees listed above that feels right to you. Ideally, the branch should be about 12 to 18 inches long and fit comfortably in your hand. Avoid taking a branch directly from a living tree unless absolutely necessary; instead, look for fallen branches that still hold energy.

2. Preparing the Wood

    - Begin by stripping the bark from the branch if desired. Use a knife or carving tools to carefully remove the bark, revealing the smooth wood underneath. If you prefer, you can leave some or all of the bark intact for a more rustic look.

3. Shaping the Wand

    - Use sandpaper to smooth the surface of the wood, starting with a coarse grit and gradually moving to a finer grit. If you wish to carve symbols, runes, or designs into the wand, use your knife or carving tools to do so carefully. These symbols can represent your intentions, personal power, or protective signs.

4. Finishing the Wand

    - Once you are satisfied with the shape and smoothness of your wand, apply a coat of beeswax or wood polish to protect the wood and enhance its natural beauty. Rub the beeswax or polish into the wood with a soft cloth, allowing it to absorb and seal the wood. Buff the wand to a soft shine.

5. Adding Decorations (Optional)

    - If you wish to add crystals, stones, or other decorations to your wand, use glue to attach them securely. Choose decorations that resonate with your intentions and the energy you want to channel through your wand. For example, you might add an amethyst crystal for clarity and protection or wrap the handle with a ribbon in your favorite color for added personal significance.

6. Charging Your Wand

    - Hold your completed wand in your hands and close your eyes. Focus on your intention and visualize the energy of Osanyin and the Magician archetype flowing into the wand. Imagine the wand glowing with a transformative light, ready to channel your personal power. Speak your intention aloud, affirming the purpose of the wand.

7. Using and Storing the Wand

   - Use your wand in rituals, spell work, or meditation to direct energy and manifest your intentions. When not in use, store the wand in a small cloth pouch or wrap it in a piece of cloth to protect it. Keep it in a sacred space, such as an altar or a special drawer, where it will be respected and cared for.

Explanation:
Crafting a wand is a powerful exercise in aligning with the transformative energy of Osanyin and the Magician archetype. The process of selecting, shaping, and charging the wand helps to focus your intention and channel positive energies towards your goals. Each step of the creation process connects you with the natural world and your personal power, fostering a sense of empowerment and transformation. By using your wand in rituals and spell work, you can harness its energy to support your journey of personal growth and change.

These exercises and rituals provide meaningful ways to connect with Osanyin and the Magician archetype, encouraging positive transformation and the channeling of energies in productive and empowering ways.

REFLECTIONS

The journey of understanding Osanyin as the Magician archetype reveals the profound depths of transformation, wisdom, and healing inherent in this powerful orisha. Through the intricate weave of mythology and spiritual practices, Osanyin stands as a testament to the enduring power of nature and the mysteries it holds. His mastery over the plant kingdom and his role as a healer and guide offer invaluable lessons for those who seek to harness their inner power and transform their lives.

Engaging with the Magician archetype through Osanyin encourages a profound connection to the natural world and the hidden energies that govern it. The stories and rituals associated with Osanyin provide a pathway to unlocking deeper levels of understanding and personal growth. By embracing the teachings of Osanyin, individuals can learn to navigate the complexities of life with greater insight and resilience.

As you incorporate the exercises and rituals inspired by Osanyin into your spiritual practice, remember the delicate balance between mastery and manipulation, power and humility. The Magician archetype, embodied by Osanyin, calls upon you to use your knowledge and abilities for the greater good, transforming not only yourself but also the world around you. Through this alignment, you can achieve a harmonious integration of the Magician's energies, fostering both personal and collective healing.

Chapter 14

The Ruler

The Ruler archetype is defined by its inherent qualities of leadership, responsibility, and control. Those who embody this archetype possess a natural ability to organize and direct others, often finding themselves in positions of power and authority. They are driven by a desire to create order, establish stability, and ensure the smooth functioning of systems and institutions. Rulers are often seen as protectors and guardians, responsible for the well-being of their community or domain. Their vision is typically long-term, focusing on the greater good and the maintenance of harmony and justice.

Rulers exhibit a commanding presence and exude confidence, which inspires trust and respect in others. Their ability to make decisive judgments and their unwavering commitment to their responsibilities are key traits that set them apart. They are often seen as wise and judicious, capable of navigating complex situations with a steady hand. The Ruler's influence is pervasive, impacting various aspects of society, from governance and politics to business and community leadership.

Strengths and Weaknesses
The strengths of the Ruler archetype lie in their capacity for strategic thinking, their organizational skills, and their ability to inspire and motivate others. Rulers are adept at seeing the big picture and making decisions that benefit the collective. Their sense of duty and commitment to their role often leads to the creation of structured and efficient systems. They are also skilled at delegating tasks and empowering others to fulfill their potential.

However, the Ruler archetype also has its weaknesses. The pursuit of control and order can sometimes lead to rigidity and inflexibility. Rulers may become overly authoritative, imposing their will on others and stifling creativity and innovation. The desire to maintain power can result in a reluctance to share authority or listen to alternative perspectives, leading to tyranny and oppression. It is essential for those embodying the Ruler archetype to balance their authoritative tendencies with humility and openness to ensure they do not become despotic.

Cultural Examples
The Ruler archetype is prominently featured in literature, film, and mythology, often depicted through characters who wield significant power and influence. One classic example is King Arthur from Arthurian legends, who embodies the ideals of chivalry, justice, and leadership. As the ruler of Camelot, King Arthur's vision of a just and fair kingdom, symbolized by the Round Table, reflects the positive aspects of the Ruler archetype. His wisdom, bravery, and commitment to his people illustrate the ideal qualities of a benevolent leader.

In modern film, characters like Mufasa from Disney's *The Lion King* represent the Ruler archetype. Mufasa's leadership is marked by his strength, wisdom, and sense of responsibility towards his kingdom. He teaches his son, Simba, about the delicate balance of life and the importance of leadership, embodying the virtues of the Ruler while also highlighting the consequences of neglecting these responsibilities.

Mythological figures such as Zeus from Greek mythology also exemplify the Ruler archetype. As the king of the gods, Zeus exercises control over the heavens and the earth, enforcing order and justice among both mortals and deities. While his rule is characterized by power and authority, Zeus's actions also demonstrate the potential for abuse of power and the importance of balance and fairness in leadership.

Historical or Contemporary Figures
Queen Elizabeth I (1533–1603)
Queen Elizabeth I of England embodies the Ruler archetype through her leadership during a period of political turmoil and cultural flourishing. Her reign, known as the Elizabethan Era, was marked by the strengthening of England's power and influence, as well as the flourishing of the arts. Elizabeth's ability to maintain control and guide her nation through challenges demonstrates the Ruler's qualities of authority, responsibility, and vision.

Nelson Mandela (1918–2013)
Nelson Mandela, the former President of South Africa and anti-apartheid revolutionary, also exemplifies the Ruler archetype. Mandela's leadership in the struggle against apartheid, his commitment to justice, and his efforts to unite a divided nation after decades of racial oppression highlight the Ruler's potential for wise and compassionate governance.

In Psychology
The Ruler archetype also plays a crucial role in the field of psychology, where it is associated with the development of personal authority and self-mastery. Jungian therapy often explores the Ruler archetype as part of the individuation process, helping individuals to develop a sense of inner control and leadership in their own lives. In organizational psychology, the Ruler

archetype is relevant in discussions about leadership styles, decision-making, and the dynamics of power within groups. The Ruler's influence is evident in the emphasis on leadership development and the growing interest in ethical and transformational leadership practices. This archetype reminds us of the importance of responsible and compassionate leadership in creating a just and orderly society.

Shadow Side
The shadow side of the Ruler archetype emerges when the desire for control and authority becomes excessive, leading to tyranny and despotism. Rulers may become consumed by their need for power, resorting to manipulation and coercion to maintain their position. This can result in the suppression of dissent and the marginalization of those who challenge their authority. The rigid enforcement of rules and expectations can stifle creativity and innovation, creating an environment of fear and compliance rather than one of growth and development.

The shadow Ruler is also prone to arrogance and hubris, believing themselves to be infallible and above reproach. This can lead to a disconnect from the needs and concerns of others, as the Ruler becomes more focused on their own interests and maintaining their dominance. The challenge for those embodying the Ruler archetype is to recognize and address these tendencies, striving for a leadership style that is inclusive, compassionate, and responsive to the needs of their community.

Path to Individuation
Balancing and integrating the Ruler archetype involves cultivating self-awareness and humility. It requires a willingness to listen to others, to share power, and to embrace a collaborative approach to leadership. The Ruler must learn to balance their need for control with flexibility and adaptability, recognizing that true strength lies in empowering others and fostering an environment of mutual respect and cooperation.

Engaging in reflective practices, such as meditation or journaling, can help the Ruler gain insight into their motivations and behaviors, allowing them to address their shadow tendencies. Seeking feedback from trusted advisors and peers can also provide valuable perspectives and help the Ruler stay grounded in their role. By embracing a leadership style that values inclusivity, empathy, and shared responsibility, the Ruler can achieve a harmonious integration of their archetype, leading with wisdom and integrity.

OBATALA AS THE RULER

Obatala, one of the most revered orishas in Yoruba mythology, exemplifies the Ruler archetype through his role as the deity of wisdom, purity, and justice. Known as the "King of the White Cloth," Obatala is often depicted as a wise and benevolent leader, responsible for the creation of humanity and the maintenance of order and harmony in the world. His attributes and stories reflect the essential qualities of the Ruler archetype, making him a fitting embodiment of this role.

Characteristics and Traits
As the orisha of wisdom and purity, Obatala embodies the qualities of leadership, responsibility, and control. He is revered for his wisdom and fair judgment, often called upon to resolve disputes and restore harmony. Obatala's commitment to justice and his ability to create order from chaos are central to his role as the Ruler. His leadership is marked by compassion, patience, and a deep sense of responsibility towards his creations and the world.

Obatala's association with the color white symbolizes his purity and clarity of vision. He is often depicted as a calm and serene figure, embodying the ideals of peace and tranquility. This serenity allows him to make balanced and fair decisions, guiding his followers with a steady hand and an open heart. His role as a creator and protector highlights his deep commitment to the well-being of humanity and the natural world.

Strengths and Weaknesses
Obatala's strengths as the Ruler are evident in his wisdom, fairness, and ability to maintain order. His decisions are guided by a sense of justice and compassion, ensuring that his leadership benefits the collective. Obatala's patience and calm demeanor enable him to navigate complex situations with grace and insight, fostering an environment of trust and respect.

However, Obatala's commitment to purity and order can also become a weakness. His desire for perfection may lead to rigidity and an intolerance for mistakes or deviations from the norm. This can create an environment of strict adherence to rules, stifling creativity and individual expression. Additionally, Obatala's serene and detached nature may sometimes be perceived as aloofness, distancing him from the emotional needs of his followers.

Cultural Examples
In Yoruba mythology, Obatala's stories illustrate his role as a wise and just ruler. One well-known tale involves Obatala's creation of humanity. According to the myth, Obatala was tasked by Olodumare, the supreme deity, with shaping human beings from clay. However, during his work, Obatala became intoxicated with palm wine and created imperfect beings. Upon realizing his mistake, he vowed to protect and care for those he had created, exemplifying his sense of responsibility and compassion.

Another story highlights Obatala's role in maintaining harmony. When conflicts arise among the orishas, Obatala is often called upon to mediate and restore balance. His wisdom and fairness ensure that disputes are resolved justly, reinforcing his position as a respected leader.

Shadow Side
The shadow side of Obatala as the Ruler archetype emerges when his pursuit of purity and order becomes excessive. His intolerance for imperfection can

lead to harsh judgment and a lack of empathy for those who do not meet his standards. This rigid adherence to rules can create an oppressive environment, where creativity and individuality are suppressed.

Additionally, Obatala's serene and detached nature may sometimes result in emotional distance from his followers. This can create a sense of isolation and disconnection, undermining the trust and respect he seeks to foster. To balance these tendencies, Obatala must cultivate humility and empathy, recognizing the value of diverse perspectives and the importance of emotional connection.

Path to Individuation
Balancing and integrating the Ruler archetype within Obatala involves embracing flexibility and compassion. By recognizing the strengths and limitations of his leadership style, Obatala can strive for a more inclusive and empathetic approach. This requires a willingness to listen to others, to share power, and to embrace the imperfections that make each individual unique.

Engaging in reflective practices, such as meditation or seeking counsel from trusted advisors, can help Obatala gain insight into his motivations and behaviors. By fostering an environment of mutual respect and collaboration, Obatala can achieve a harmonious integration of the Ruler archetype, leading with wisdom and integrity. Through this balanced approach, he can continue to guide and protect his followers, ensuring the well-being of his community and the natural world.

OBATALA STORIES

One of the most well-known stories involving Obatala is his creation of humanity. Tasked by Olodumare to mold humans from clay, Obatala set about his work with great care. However, he grew weary and, in a moment of distraction, drank palm wine. Under its influence, he shaped some imperfect figures. Upon realizing what he had done, Obatala vowed to protect and care for those he had created, embracing his responsibility as their creator. This story emphasizes his compassion and sense of duty, as well as his commitment to rectifying his mistakes and ensuring the well-being of all his creations.

Another significant tale involves Obatala's journey to a mountain to meditate and seek wisdom. During this journey, he encountered various challenges and temptations but remained steadfast in his purpose. This story underscores Obatala's dedication to self-improvement and his pursuit of spiritual enlightenment, highlighting his role as a guide and mentor to others.

In another narrative, Obatala demonstrates his wisdom and fairness in a dispute between two towns over a boundary line. Called upon to mediate, Obatala listened to both sides and then proposed a solution that was fair and just, ensuring that both towns could coexist peacefully. This tale illustrates his abilities as a mediator and his commitment to justice, reinforcing his reputation as a wise and impartial leader.

One lesser-known story speaks of Obatala's encounter with a deceitful spirit who tried to trick him into giving up his powers. The spirit disguised itself as a needy traveler and asked Obatala for help. Sensing the deceit, Obatala remained calm and offered genuine assistance, which revealed the spirit's true nature. This story highlights Obatala's discernment and his ability to see through deception, reinforcing his status as a protector of truth and integrity.

These stories collectively showcase Obatala's multifaceted character—his wisdom, compassion, dedication to justice, and his occasional susceptibility to human flaws. They offer a rich tapestry of lessons and insights, demonstrating why Obatala is revered as a central figure in Yoruba cosmology and why he is fittingly aligned with the Ruler archetype.

EXERCISES & RITUALS

Peace and Clarity Ritual Inspired by Eborí Eledá

Disclaimer: This ritual is designed for use by non-initiates and is not the exact same as the ones performed by ordained priests within Yoruba or Lukumi traditions. It is intended to provide a sense of peace and clarity of mind in a manner that respects and acknowledges the deeper spiritual practices of these traditions.

<u>Supplies Needed</u>:
- A fresh coconut
- Cotton balls
- A bowl of cool water
- A white cloth or towel
- A quiet space for meditation

<u>Guidelines</u>:

1. Preparation:
    - Find a quiet, comfortable space where you will not be disturbed. Ensure the area is clean and free from distractions.
    - Gather all the supplies and place them within reach. Break open the fresh coconut, collecting the coconut water in a bowl.

2. Cleansing:
    - Begin by cleansing yourself mentally and emotionally. Sit quietly, close your eyes, and take a few deep breaths to center yourself.
    - Imagine any negative thoughts, worries, or stresses being released with each exhale, and positive, calming energy entering with each inhale.

3. Application of Coconut Water:
   - Dip your fingers into the bowl of coconut water. Gently dab the coconut water onto your forehead, the crown of your head, and the back of your head.
   - As you apply the coconut water, silently affirm your intention for peace and clarity. For example, you might say, "May my mind be clear and my spirit be at peace."

4. Cotton Placement:
   - Take the cotton balls and moisten them slightly with the cool water. Place the moistened cotton balls on the same areas where you applied the coconut water: the forehead, crown, and back of the head.
   - Cover your head with the white cloth or towel, allowing the cotton balls to remain in place. This symbolizes the absorption of peace and clarity into your mind and spirit.

5. Meditation:
   - Sit or lie down comfortably with the white cloth or towel covering your head. Close your eyes and focus on your breath, maintaining a slow and steady rhythm.
   - Visualize a bright white light surrounding your head, filling your mind with tranquility and clarity. Imagine this light dissolving any remaining tension or confusion.

6. Reflection:
   - After meditating for at least 10-15 minutes, gently remove the white cloth or towel and the cotton balls. Take a moment to reflect on how you feel and any insights that may have come to you during the meditation.
   - Write down any thoughts, feelings, or messages in a journal, if desired.

7. Completion:
   - Thank the elements (the coconut, cotton, and water) for their role in your ritual. Dispose of the used cotton balls in a respectful manner, such as burying them in the earth or placing them in a natural body of water.
   - Wash your face and head with cool water to finalize the cleansing process.

Benefits:
This ritual promotes mental clarity and peace by combining the soothing properties of coconut water with the symbolic purification of cotton. It encourages deep relaxation, introspection, and a sense of renewal. By regularly practicing this ritual, you can cultivate a clearer, more focused mind and a peaceful spirit, aiding in your alignment with the Ruler archetype.

This adapted ritual honors the essence of traditional practices while being accessible and respectful to those who are not initiated into specific spiritual lineages.

Creating a Sacred Space for Reflection

Supplies Needed:
- White cloth or fabric
- Candles (preferably white)
- Incense (frankincense or myrrh)
- A journal and pen
- A comfortable cushion or chair

Guidelines:
Begin by setting up a sacred space in a quiet area of your home. Spread the white cloth on a table or the floor, symbolizing purity and clarity. Place the candles and incense on the cloth and light them, inviting a serene and

meditative atmosphere. Sit comfortably on the cushion or chair, with the journal and pen in front of you.

Focus on your breath, allowing yourself to relax and become present. Reflect on your role as a leader in your own life and consider the responsibilities and decisions you face. Write down any thoughts, feelings, or insights that arise, acknowledging both your strengths and areas for growth.

This ritual helps to center your mind, fostering clarity and a deeper connection to the qualities of leadership and responsibility. It encourages introspection and self-awareness, essential traits for balancing the Ruler archetype.

Crafting a Leadership Symbol

Supplies Needed:
- Clay or sculpting material
- Paint and brushes
- A small piece of wood or stone

Guidelines:
Create a physical symbol of your leadership qualities by crafting an object that represents your values and vision. Using clay or sculpting material, form a shape that resonates with your idea of leadership—this could be a staff, a crown, or a symbol of balance and justice.

Once you have sculpted the shape, paint it with colors and designs that reflect your leadership qualities. For example, white to symbolize purity and clarity, gold for wisdom, or blue for calmness and stability. Place this symbol in your workspace or a prominent place in your home as a constant reminder of your commitment to leading with integrity and responsibility.

THE RULER

Honoring the Ancestors and Seeking Guidance

Supplies Needed:
- An ancestral altar (a small table or shelf)
- Photos or mementos of ancestors
- Offerings (such as fruits, flowers, or water)
- A white candle
- A bowl of water and a small cloth

Guidelines:
Create an ancestral altar by placing photos or mementos of your ancestors on a small table or shelf. Add offerings such as fruits, flowers, or water to honor their memory. Light the white candle, symbolizing purity and connection to the divine.

Sit quietly in front of the altar and place your hands over the bowl of water. Focus on your ancestors, inviting their wisdom and guidance into your life. Use the cloth to gently sprinkle water around the altar, symbolizing the cleansing and purifying influence of Obatala.

Speak aloud or silently, asking for guidance and support in your role as a leader. Express gratitude for the wisdom and strength passed down through generations. This ritual helps to connect you with your lineage, fostering a sense of continuity and grounding your leadership in the values and lessons of your ancestors.

Vision Board for Leadership and Clarity

Supplies Needed:
- A large piece of poster board or a corkboard
- Magazines, photos, and printed images
- Scissors, glue, and push pins
- Markers or pens

Guidelines:
Create a vision board focused on leadership, clarity, and responsibility. Begin by cutting out images and words from magazines that resonate with your vision of effective leadership and the qualities you wish to embody. Arrange the images on the board, using glue or push pins to secure them in place.

Include representations of your goals, values, and inspirations. Use markers or pens to write affirmations or quotes that reinforce your commitment to positive leadership. Place the vision board in a prominent location where you will see it daily.

This exercise helps to clarify your intentions and keep you focused on your goals. It serves as a visual reminder of the qualities and values you strive to embody, reinforcing your connection to the Ruler archetype and the guiding influence of Obatala.

These exercises and rituals provide a structured approach to aligning with Obatala and the Ruler archetype. By incorporating these practices into your daily life, you can cultivate the qualities of leadership, responsibility, and control, while also addressing the shadow side of the archetype. These activities promote self-awareness, community engagement, and a deeper connection to the wisdom and guidance of Obatala.

REFLECTIONS

Obatala's embodiment of the Ruler archetype offers a profound template for understanding leadership rooted in wisdom, compassion, and ethical responsibility. Through his narratives and attributes, we see how true leadership is not about dominance or control, but about guiding others with a fair and just hand, maintaining a vision of harmony and balance. His stories, whether creating humanity or mediating disputes, highlight the delicate balance between authority and empathy, showcasing the depth of his character and the breadth of his influence.

The exercises and rituals presented in this chapter serve as practical tools for aligning oneself with these qualities, promoting self-reflection, ethical decision-making, and a sense of community. By embracing these practices, individuals can cultivate a leadership style that is both strong and compassionate, resilient and adaptable.

Obatala's legacy teaches us that the path of the Ruler is one of continuous growth, self-awareness, and a deep commitment to the well-being of all. As we integrate these lessons into our lives, we can aspire to lead with the same grace and integrity, becoming beacons of wisdom and justice in our own right.

Chapter 15

The Martyr

This ***bonus*** chapter introduces the Martyr archetype, a profound symbol of self-sacrifice, devotion, and resilience. While not included in the traditional twelve Jungian archetypes, the Martyr occupies a unique space that blends elements of both the Hero and the Caregiver archetypes. This archetype resonates deeply with the themes of empathy and the transformative power of sacrifice, making it worthy of focused exploration. Through a detailed examination of the Martyr archetype's characteristics, strengths, weaknesses, cultural examples, shadow side, and path to individuation, we gain insight into this archetype's role in personal and collective narratives. Obba Nani, a significant figure in Yoruba mythology, serves as a poignant example of the Martyr archetype and provides a rich context for understanding its dynamics.

Characteristics and Traits

The Martyr archetype is characterized by an intrinsic drive to serve others, often at great personal cost. Individuals embodying this archetype prioritize the welfare of others over their own, motivated by a deep sense of moral obligation and compassion. Martyrs are typically seen as selfless individuals who willingly endure hardships to protect and support their loved ones, communities, or causes they are passionate about.

A key trait of the Martyr is their unwavering devotion to a cause or person. This devotion often manifests as a willingness to make significant sacrifices, driven by an empathetic understanding of the needs and suffering of others. The Martyr's strength lies in their ability to connect deeply with those they serve, drawing on their empathy to inspire and uplift others through their actions. They possess a keen awareness of the transformative potential of sacrifice, recognizing that their efforts can lead to meaningful change and healing.

However, the Martyr's inclination towards self-sacrifice can also become a source of conflict. While their dedication is commendable, it often comes at the expense of their own well-being. Martyrs may neglect their personal needs, leading to physical and emotional exhaustion. This duality highlights the importance of balance within the Martyr archetype, as individuals must learn to navigate their desire to serve with their own self-care.

Strengths and Weaknesses
The strengths of the Martyr archetype are rooted in their capacity for empathy, compassion, and resilience. Martyrs inspire those around them through their selfless actions, demonstrating the power of love and sacrifice to bring about positive change. Their dedication to others fosters a sense of solidarity and community, encouraging others to join in their efforts and act with kindness and understanding.

The Martyr's resilience is a significant strength, as they possess the ability to endure and persevere through adversity. This endurance is often fueled by their unwavering commitment to their cause, allowing them to overcome obstacles and remain steadfast in their pursuit of justice and healing. Martyrs are often seen as role models, embodying the ideals of courage and selflessness in the face of hardship.

THE MARTYR

However, the Martyr's strengths can also become their weaknesses. The tendency to prioritize others above themselves can lead to burnout, as Martyrs may push themselves beyond their limits in their quest to help others. This cycle of sacrifice and depletion can result in physical and emotional exhaustion, diminishing their ability to serve effectively. Additionally, Martyrs may struggle with feelings of resentment or frustration if their efforts are not acknowledged or appreciated, leading to a sense of isolation or martyrdom.

To navigate these challenges, Martyrs must cultivate self-awareness and learn to balance their selfless nature with self-care. By setting healthy boundaries and recognizing their own needs, Martyrs can sustain their capacity to serve others without sacrificing their well-being.

Cultural Examples
In literature and film, the Martyr archetype is often portrayed through characters who willingly endure suffering, sacrifice, or even death for a greater cause, reflecting the universal theme of self-sacrifice. These characters exemplify the Martyr's deep commitment to their principles, often at great personal cost, inspiring others through their ultimate acts of devotion.

One of the most powerful literary examples of the Martyr archetype is Sydney Carton from Charles Dickens' *A Tale of Two Cities*. Sydney Carton, a dissipated lawyer who struggles with his sense of purpose and self-worth, finds redemption through an act of profound sacrifice. In a dramatic turn of events, Carton takes the place of his lookalike, Charles Darnay, who is condemned to die during the French Revolution. Carton's famous final words, "It is a far, far better thing that I do, than I have ever done," capture the essence of the Martyr archetype—an individual who attains spiritual redemption by giving up his life for the happiness and safety of others. His sacrifice is both a personal and moral victory, transforming his life of wasted potential into a powerful narrative of selflessness and love.

In film, the character of Obi-Wan Kenobi from the *Star Wars* saga is another good example of the Martyr archetype. As a wise and noble Jedi Master, Obi-Wan dedicates his life to the protection and training of the young Luke Skywalker, guiding him on his path to becoming a Jedi. Obi-Wan's ultimate act of martyrdom occurs in *Star Wars: A New Hope* when he faces his former apprentice, Darth Vader, in a final duel. Understanding that his death will inspire Luke and strengthen the Rebel Alliance, Obi-Wan sacrifices himself, allowing Vader to strike him down. This act not only exemplifies the Martyr's willingness to give up everything for a greater cause but also demonstrates how martyrdom can serve as a catalyst for greater victories, as Obi-Wan's spirit continues to guide Luke from beyond.

Another compelling portrayal of the Martyr archetype in film is John Proctor in Arthur Miller's *The Crucible*, which has been adapted into several films. Set during the Salem witch trials, Proctor is a man of integrity who becomes entangled in the hysteria that grips the town. Accused of witchcraft, Proctor refuses to falsely confess, even though doing so would save his life. His decision to die rather than live a lie serves as a powerful statement against the corrupt judicial system and the mass hysteria of the time. Proctor's sacrifice is a poignant reminder of the Martyr's strength in standing up for truth and justice, even in the face of death.

Aslan, the majestic lion from *The Chronicles of Narnia* series by C.S. Lewis, is another iconic representation of the Martyr archetype. In *The Lion, the Witch, and the Wardrobe*, Aslan willingly sacrifices himself to save Edmund Pevensie, who has betrayed his siblings and fallen under the spell of the White Witch. Aslan's death on the Stone Table is a selfless act of atonement, embodying the Martyr's role as a savior who takes on the burden of others' sins. His subsequent resurrection symbolizes the power of self-sacrifice to bring about renewal and hope, reinforcing the Martyr's deep spiritual significance.

THE MARTYR

These characters from literature and film embody the Martyr archetype through their profound acts of self-sacrifice, reflecting the timeless theme of enduring suffering for a cause greater than oneself. Through their stories, we see the Martyr's ability to inspire, uplift, and bring about transformative change, whether in personal redemption, societal justice, or spiritual renewal.

Historical or Contemporary Figures
Joan of Arc (c. 1412–1431)
Joan of Arc, a French heroine and Catholic saint, is a quintessential example of the Martyr archetype. Her conviction in her divine mission led her to fight for France during the Hundred Years' War, ultimately leading to her capture and execution. Joan's willingness to sacrifice her life for her beliefs and her country embodies the essence of the Martyr, making her an enduring symbol of courage and faith.

Emily Davison (1872–1913)
Emily Davison, the British suffragette who fought for women's right to vote, also represents the Martyr archetype. Davison's activism, including her ultimate sacrifice at the Epsom Derby, highlights the Martyr's drive for justice and the willingness to endure suffering for a cause. Her legacy continues to inspire those who fight for equality and human rights.

In Psychology
The Martyr archetype is also relevant in modern psychology, where it is associated with the concepts of altruism, empathy, and resilience. Therapists may work with clients to explore the Martyr archetype as a way of understanding their motivations for helping others, as well as the potential dangers of self-sacrifice and burnout. The Martyr's influence is evident in the growing emphasis on social responsibility, volunteerism, and the ethical dimensions of leadership. This archetype reminds us of the profound impact that selfless individuals can have on the world, as well as the importance of balancing compassion with self-care to avoid the pitfalls of martyrdom.

Shadow Side

The shadow side of the Martyr archetype can manifest in various ways, often stemming from the challenges associated with excessive self-sacrifice and neglect of personal needs. While the Martyr's dedication to others is commendable, it can lead to an unhealthy neglect of their own well-being, resulting in physical and emotional exhaustion.

One aspect of the Martyr's shadow side is the tendency towards self-neglect, as individuals may become so focused on serving others that they overlook their own needs. This self-neglect can lead to burnout, diminishing their ability to help others effectively. Over time, the Martyr's health and well-being may suffer, resulting in physical illness or emotional distress.

Another manifestation of the shadow side is the potential for resentment and frustration if the Martyr's efforts are not recognized or appreciated. This sense of unacknowledged sacrifice can lead to bitterness and a perception of being taken for granted. Martyrs may develop a martyr complex, where they seek validation and purpose through their suffering, potentially alienating themselves from those they seek to help.

To address the shadow side of the Martyr archetype, individuals must cultivate self-compassion and embrace the importance of self-care. By acknowledging their own needs and setting boundaries, Martyrs can sustain their capacity to serve others while maintaining their physical and emotional health. This balance allows them to continue their work without falling into the traps of burnout and resentment.

Path to Individuation

The path to individuation for the Martyr archetype involves integrating their selfless nature with a healthy sense of self-care and balance. Martyrs must learn to recognize their own needs and to prioritize their well-being alongside their desire to serve others. This journey requires cultivating self-awareness and setting boundaries to prevent burnout and resentment.

THE MARTYR

For Martyrs, individuation involves embracing the transformative power of their empathy and compassion while acknowledging the importance of self-care. This process encourages Martyrs to find a balance between serving others and nurturing their own physical and emotional health, allowing them to sustain their capacity to help others without sacrificing their well-being.

One aspect of the individuation process for Martyrs is learning to set healthy boundaries, ensuring that their self-sacrificial tendencies do not lead to self-neglect. This involves recognizing when to say no and understanding that self-care is not selfish but essential for sustaining their ability to serve. By practicing self-compassion and embracing their worth, Martyrs can achieve a harmonious integration of their selfless nature and their personal well-being.

Additionally, the path to individuation involves finding meaning and purpose beyond sacrifice. Martyrs must explore their values and passions, seeking fulfillment in areas that nourish their souls and contribute to their growth. By aligning their actions with their authentic selves, Martyrs can transcend the limitations of the archetype and achieve a sense of wholeness and balance.

Through this process of self-discovery and integration, Martyrs can realize their full potential, transforming their capacity for sacrifice into a powerful force for positive change. By balancing their selflessness with self-care, Martyrs can continue to inspire and uplift others while maintaining their own health and well-being.

OBBA NANI AS THE MARTYR

Obba Nani, also known simply as Obba, is a prominent figure in Yoruba mythology, embodying the Martyr archetype through her story of love, sacrifice, and resilience. As the wife of Shango, the orisha of thunder and lightning, Obba's narrative is marked by her unwavering devotion and willingness to endure hardship for the sake of her husband.

Connection to the Martyr Archetype

Obba's story begins with her deep love and commitment to Shango. Her willingness to go to great lengths to please him highlights her selfless nature and her desire to serve those she loves. This devotion is exemplified in the tragic tale of her sacrifice, where she cuts off her own ear to prove her love and loyalty to Shango. This act, though misguided, underscores the Martyr's capacity for self-sacrifice and their deep sense of empathy and compassion.

Strengths and Weaknesses

Obba's strengths as a Martyr are evident in her capacity for love, empathy, and resilience. Her willingness to endure pain and suffering for the sake of her loved ones exemplifies the Martyr's transformative power. However, her story also highlights the weaknesses of the Martyr archetype. Obba's excessive self-sacrifice leads to her downfall, illustrating the dangers of neglecting one's own needs and the potential for resentment and isolation.

Obba's narrative demonstrates the Martyr's ability to inspire through selfless actions, as her love and dedication to Shango are central to her identity. However, her story also serves as a cautionary tale, highlighting the importance of balance and self-care. By neglecting her own needs, Obba becomes vulnerable to the shadow side of the Martyr archetype, ultimately leading to her suffering and isolation.

Cultural Significance

Obba Nani's narrative holds significant cultural importance within Yoruba mythology, offering a rich context for exploring the Martyr archetype. Her story resonates with universal themes of love, sacrifice, and the complexities of devotion, providing valuable insights into the Martyr's role in both personal and collective contexts.

THE MARTYR

In Yoruba culture, Obba's story is often interpreted as a lesson in the complexities of love and sacrifice. Her actions serve as a reminder of the potential dangers of unchecked selflessness and the importance of setting healthy boundaries. Her narrative highlights the cultural significance of balance and self-care, emphasizing the need for individuals to care for themselves as they care for others.

Shadow Side

The shadow side of Obba's story is reflected in her extreme self-sacrifice and the resulting emotional and physical harm. Her actions, driven by a desire to please and serve, ultimately lead to her suffering and isolation. This narrative serves as a powerful reminder of the importance of balance and self-care, highlighting the potential dangers of unchecked martyrdom.

Obba's story illustrates the potential for resentment and frustration if sacrifices go unrecognized or unappreciated. Her willingness to sacrifice for Shango's love leads to feelings of betrayal and despair, underscoring the need for Martyrs to recognize their worth and to set boundaries that protect their well-being.

Path to Individuation

Obba Nani's journey offers valuable lessons for Martyrs on the path to individuation. Her story underscores the need for balance, self-awareness, and the importance of setting healthy boundaries. By embracing these lessons, Martyrs can achieve a harmonious integration of their selfless nature and their personal well-being, allowing them to serve others more effectively and sustainably.

For Obba, individuation involves recognizing the value of self-care and the importance of maintaining her own identity alongside her devotion to others. Her story highlights the need for Martyrs to balance their selfless nature with personal well-being, ensuring that their sacrifices do not lead to burnout or isolation.

By integrating these lessons, Martyrs can achieve a harmonious balance between their selfless nature and their personal well-being, allowing them to serve others more effectively and sustainably. This journey of self-discovery and integration enables Martyrs to realize their full potential, transforming their capacity for sacrifice into a powerful force for positive change.

The exploration of Obba as the Martyr archetype highlights the profound impact of love and sacrifice in both personal and cultural contexts. By understanding her story and the lessons it imparts, individuals can cultivate a deeper appreciation for the Martyr archetype and its enduring significance in the human experience.

OBBA STORIES

Obba's stories often highlight themes of sacrifice, loyalty, and the complexities of love and relationships. Beyond the well-known tale of her tragic sacrifice involving the loss of her ear, her narratives provide further insights into her role and significance within Yoruba mythology.

Obba Nani and Her Sacred River
One of the most prominent stories of Obba pertains to her association with the Oba River. According to Yoruba mythology, Obba is the guardian of this sacred river, which bears her name. The river is considered a symbol of her enduring spirit and the purity of her love and sacrifice. It is said that the river's waters are imbued with healing properties, reflecting Obba's nurturing and protective nature.

The story of Obba and her river highlights her resilience and strength. After her tragic sacrifice and subsequent rejection by Shango, she sought solace in the waters of her river. It was here that she transformed her sorrow into a source of strength, using the river as a sanctuary for healing and renewal.

This narrative emphasizes the Martyr archetype's ability to find resilience in adversity, transforming pain into empowerment.

Obba's connection to the river is celebrated in various rituals and ceremonies. Devotees often visit the Oba River to pay homage to her and seek her blessings for love, healing, and protection. The river serves as a testament to her enduring legacy and her role as a guardian of the faithful.

Obba Nani's Wisdom and Guidance
In addition to her role as a loving and devoted wife, Obba is revered for her wisdom and guidance. In Yoruba mythology, she is often depicted as a wise counselor who offers guidance and support to those in need. Her insights and advice are sought by individuals seeking clarity and direction in their lives, particularly in matters of the heart and relationships.

One story highlights Obba's role as a mediator in disputes among the orisha. When tensions arose between Shango and his brother Ogun, the orisha of iron and war, she played a crucial role in facilitating reconciliation. Her ability to empathize with both sides and her diplomatic approach allowed her to mediate effectively, fostering understanding and harmony among the orisha. This narrative underscores the Martyr's capacity for empathy and their ability to bring about healing and resolution through their compassionate nature.

Obba's wisdom is also evident in her teachings about the importance of balance in relationships. She advocates for mutual respect and understanding, emphasizing the need for partners to support one another while maintaining their individuality. Her teachings resonate with those who seek guidance in navigating the complexities of love and commitment, offering valuable insights into the dynamics of healthy and harmonious relationships.

Obba Nani's Influence in Healing and Protection

Another significant aspect of Obba's story is her influence in healing and protection. As a nurturing and compassionate figure, she is often called upon for her protective qualities and her ability to provide comfort and solace to those in distress. Her presence is felt in the healing rituals and ceremonies conducted by her devotees, who seek her blessings for physical, emotional, and spiritual well-being.

In one story, Obba is credited with saving a village from a devastating illness. When a mysterious plague swept through the community, causing suffering and death, she intervened by using her knowledge of herbs and healing practices. Through her efforts, the illness was eradicated, and the village was restored to health and prosperity. This narrative highlights the Martyr's role as a healer and protector, underscoring the transformative power of compassion and selfless service.

Obba's influence in healing extends beyond physical ailments. She is also revered for her ability to heal emotional wounds and to provide strength and comfort to those experiencing grief or loss. Her presence is invoked in rituals that focus on healing broken hearts and mending fractured relationships, reflecting her enduring legacy as a symbol of love, sacrifice, and resilience.

Obba Nani's Role in the Pantheon

Obba's role within the Yoruba pantheon is multifaceted, encompassing her attributes as a loving wife, wise counselor, and compassionate healer. Her narratives provide valuable insights into the complexities of love and sacrifice, offering lessons on the importance of balance, empathy, and resilience.

As a Martyr archetype, Obba Nani embodies the transformative power of sacrifice and the ability to find strength in adversity. Her stories serve as a reminder of the enduring impact of love and devotion, highlighting the potential for individuals to effect meaningful change through their selfless actions. Through her narratives, she continues to inspire those who seek to embody the ideals of compassion, empathy, and resilience.

Obba's legacy is celebrated in various rituals and ceremonies, where devotees honor her contributions to Yoruba mythology and seek her guidance and protection. Her enduring presence within the pantheon underscores the significance of her role as a Martyr and her lasting impact on the cultural and spiritual landscape of the Yoruba people.

EXERCISES & RITUALS

Here are some exercises and rituals designed to align with Obba Nani and the Martyr archetype, focusing on overcoming the shadow aspects and channeling these energies positively and productively. Each exercise aims to cultivate self-awareness, balance, and resilience while honoring the qualities of devotion and empathy inherent in the Martyr archetype.

Reflection and Boundaries Ritual

Supplies Needed:
- Journal or notebook
- Pen
- Quiet space

Guidelines:
1. Set the Space: Find a quiet, comfortable space where you can reflect without interruptions. Light a candle or play soft music if it helps create a calming atmosphere.
2. Intention Setting: Begin by setting an intention to explore your boundaries and the balance between selflessness and self-care. Acknowledge any feelings of resentment or burnout you may have experienced due to excessive self-sacrifice.

3. Journaling Exercise: Write down the areas in your life where you feel overextended or taken for granted. Reflect on the reasons behind your self-sacrifice and how it has impacted your well-being. Consider the emotions that arise and how you might be able to address them.
4. Identifying Boundaries: List specific boundaries you would like to establish to protect your well-being and ensure balance. Consider areas where you need to say no or prioritize your own needs alongside those of others.
5. Affirmation Creation: Write down affirmations that reinforce your commitment to self-care and balance. Examples include "I am worthy of rest and rejuvenation" or "I honor my needs as I serve others." Repeat these affirmations daily to internalize the message.

Explanation:
This ritual encourages self-reflection and the establishment of healthy boundaries, allowing individuals to align with the Martyr archetype without succumbing to burnout or resentment. By acknowledging their own needs and setting boundaries, participants can channel their selfless energy positively and sustainably.

Acts of Service with Awareness

Supplies Needed:
- A list of potential acts of service (e.g., volunteering, helping a neighbor, random acts of kindness)

Guidelines:
1. Create a List: Identify various ways you can engage in acts of service, considering both small gestures and larger commitments. Choose actions that resonate with you and align with your values.
2. Intention Setting: Before engaging in an act of service, set a clear intention for your actions. Acknowledge the positive impact you hope to make and the personal fulfillment you wish to experience.

3. Mindful Engagement: Perform each act of service with full presence and awareness. Pay attention to the interactions and connections that arise, focusing on the gratitude and joy that accompany your actions.
4. Self-Reflection: After completing an act of service, take a moment to reflect on the experience. Consider the emotions it evoked and the lessons learned about the balance between giving and receiving.
5. Incorporate Regularly: Aim to incorporate acts of service into your routine, maintaining a healthy balance between giving to others and caring for yourself.

Explanation:
This exercise encourages individuals to engage in acts of service mindfully, promoting a sense of fulfillment and connection without compromising their own well-being. By aligning with the Martyr archetype in a balanced way, participants can channel their energy productively.

Healing Circle and Sharing Session

Supplies Needed:
- Group of supportive friends or community members
- Comfortable meeting space
- Talking stick or object to designate the speaker

Guidelines:
1. Gather a Group: Invite a group of supportive individuals to participate in a healing circle focused on sharing and connection. Choose a comfortable and safe space for the gathering.
2. Set the Intention: Begin by setting an intention for the circle, focusing on healing, empathy, and mutual support. Encourage participants to approach the session with openness and non-judgment.

3. Sharing Exercise: Use a talking stick or object to designate the speaker, allowing each participant to share their experiences related to self-sacrifice, compassion, and finding balance. Encourage honesty and vulnerability, creating a space for mutual understanding and empathy.
4. Collective Reflection: After everyone has had a chance to share, engage in a group reflection on the themes and insights that emerged during the session. Discuss strategies for maintaining balance and resilience while embodying the Martyr archetype.
5. Closing Ritual: Conclude the circle with a ritual of gratitude and affirmation, expressing appreciation for the connections formed and the lessons learned. Consider incorporating a closing gesture, such as holding hands or offering a collective blessing.

Explanation:
This exercise fosters a sense of community and connection, allowing individuals to share their experiences and insights related to the Martyr archetype. By engaging in collective reflection and support, participants can navigate the challenges of self-sacrifice while maintaining balance and resilience.

Heart-Centered Breathwork

Supplies Needed:
- A quiet, comfortable space
- Optional: relaxing music or a meditation app

Guidelines:
1. Set the Space: Find a comfortable place to sit or lie down, free from distractions. If you wish, play soft music or use a meditation app to enhance relaxation.

THE MARTYR

2. Focus on the Breath: Close your eyes and take a few deep breaths to center yourself. Begin to focus on your heart area, imagining each breath flowing in and out of your chest.
3. Heart-Centered Breathing: As you breathe, visualize a warm, glowing light expanding from your heart with each inhale. With each exhale, imagine the light enveloping your entire body, filling you with compassion and love.
4. Invite Healing and Balance: With each breath, invite healing and balance into your life. Release any tension or negativity, allowing the breath to cleanse and renew your spirit.
5. Reflect and Transition: After several minutes of breathwork, slowly open your eyes and take a moment to reflect on the experience. Consider how you can incorporate this sense of balance and compassion into your daily life.

Explanation:
Heart-centered breathwork helps individuals cultivate inner peace and balance, aligning with the Martyr archetype's themes of empathy and healing. This practice promotes self-awareness and resilience, enabling participants to channel their energies positively.

REFLECTIONS

The exploration of Obba Nani as the embodiment of the Martyr archetype offers profound insights into the power and complexity of self-sacrifice and devotion. Her narrative, deeply woven into Yoruba mythology, underscores the transformative impact of love and empathy, while simultaneously highlighting the potential pitfalls of unchecked selflessness. Through Obba Nani's story, we see the intricate balance required to navigate the Martyr archetype, emphasizing the necessity of self-awareness, self-care, and the establishment of healthy boundaries.

The lessons gleaned from Obba Nani's journey are both timeless and universally applicable. Her unwavering commitment to love and service is an inspiring testament to the enduring strength and resilience of the human spirit. Yet, her narrative also serves as a poignant reminder of the importance of maintaining a harmonious equilibrium between giving and receiving. The Martyr archetype challenges individuals to cultivate compassion and empathy while recognizing their inherent worth and the value of their own needs.

As we reflect on the various exercises and rituals associated with the Martyr archetype, it becomes clear that this path is one of deep introspection and intentionality. Engaging in practices that promote balance, healing, and self-awareness allows individuals to channel the Martyr's energy constructively and sustainably. By embracing these practices, one can transcend the limitations of the archetype, transforming their capacity for sacrifice into a powerful force for positive change and empowerment.

Ultimately, the story of Obba Nani and the Martyr archetype invites us to consider the profound impact of our actions on ourselves and the world around us. It challenges us to find strength in vulnerability and to use our empathy as a tool for connection and transformation. By aligning with the Martyr archetype with intention and awareness, we can cultivate a life of purpose and meaning, leaving a lasting legacy of love and compassion.

Chapter 16
Integration and Application of the Archetypes

Understanding Your Dominant Archetypes
Archetypes are universal, symbolic patterns that represent fundamental human themes. Understanding which of these patterns dominates your personality is crucial for self-awareness and personal growth. This section delves into the process of identifying and analyzing your dominant archetypes, offering practical tools for self-assessment and reflection.

Identifying your dominant archetypes begins with introspection. Reflect on the thirteen archetypes covered in this book—The Innocent, The Orphan/Everyman, The Hero, The Caregiver, The Explorer, The Rebel, The Lover, The Creator, The Jester, The Sage, The Magician, The Ruler, and The Martyr. Each archetype represents a set of behaviors, motivations, and emotional responses. Consider how these archetypes manifest in your life. For instance, if you often find yourself taking on leadership roles, guiding others with a sense of justice and fairness, you might strongly identify with the Ruler archetype. If you are driven by curiosity and a desire for adventure, the Explorer archetype may be more prominent in your personality.

Self-assessment tools such as journaling and personality tests can be instrumental in this process. Journaling allows you to track your thoughts, feelings, and actions over time, revealing patterns that correspond to specific archetypes. For example, you might notice recurring themes of nurturing and protecting others, pointing to a strong presence of the Caregiver archetype. Personality tests, while not definitive, can offer insights into your dominant traits and how they align with the archetypes.

Discussion with friends, family, or a mentor can also provide valuable perspectives. Others might see aspects of your personality that you overlook. For example, they might recognize the Sage archetype in your ability to offer wise advice, even if you don't see yourself that way. Combining these various methods of self-assessment can lead to a more comprehensive understanding of your dominant archetypes.

Once you have identified your dominant archetypes, it is essential to analyze how they influence your life. Consider how these archetypes affect your decisions, relationships, and personal growth. Are they helping you achieve your goals, or are they holding you back in some areas? Understanding your dominant archetypes provides a foundation for personal development, allowing you to harness their strengths and mitigate their challenges.

Balancing Archetypes in Everyday Life
Balancing your archetypes is a dynamic process that requires ongoing attention and adjustment. Each archetype brings with it strengths and challenges, and the goal is to integrate these influences into a balanced and harmonious personality. This section explores practical strategies for achieving this balance in your daily life.

Living in harmony with your archetypes means embracing their positive aspects while being mindful of their potential pitfalls. For example, the Hero archetype is associated with courage, determination, and a strong sense of purpose. However, if left unchecked, the Hero can also manifest as arrogance or an overwhelming need to prove oneself. To balance the Hero archetype, you might practice humility by acknowledging the contributions of others and recognizing your limitations. Setting realistic goals and boundaries can prevent burnout and ensure that your drive does not lead to self-destructive behavior.

Similarly, the Rebel archetype, with its emphasis on non-conformity and challenging the status quo, can be a powerful force for change. However, this archetype can also lead to destructiveness if not tempered with foresight and empathy. Balancing the Rebel involves cultivating patience and strategic thinking, ensuring that your actions are not only bold but also constructive and beneficial to others.

Incorporating rituals and practices that resonate with your archetypes can help maintain this balance. For instance, if the Creator archetype is dominant in your life, you might engage in regular creative activities such as writing, painting, or music. These practices allow you to express your creativity while also providing an outlet for processing emotions and thoughts. For the Sage, meditation or reading philosophical texts might be more appropriate, fostering wisdom and insight while keeping the potential for detachment in check.

Balancing your archetypes also involves being adaptable. Life circumstances change, and so too might the dominance of certain archetypes. For example, during times of crisis, the Warrior archetype might come to the forefront, driving you to protect and defend. In contrast, during periods of reflection and solitude, the Sage might take precedence. Being flexible and responsive to these shifts is key to maintaining psychological and emotional balance.

Ultimately, balancing your archetypes in everyday life is about integrating their energies in a way that supports your well-being and growth. It is a continuous process of self-reflection, adjustment, and practice, leading to a more harmonious and fulfilling life.

Archetypes in Relationships

Archetypes significantly influence our interactions with others, shaping the dynamics of our relationships. Understanding how your dominant archetypes interact with those of others can lead to more harmonious and fulfilling connections. This section explores how archetypes manifest in various types of relationships and offers strategies for navigating these dynamics effectively.

In romantic relationships, complementary archetypes often create a balance that strengthens the bond between partners. For example, a relationship between a Lover and a Caregiver can be deeply nurturing, with each partner bringing emotional warmth and support to the other. The Lover's passion and desire for connection complement the Caregiver's instinct to nurture and protect, creating a relationship built on mutual affection and care. However, when archetypes clash, conflicts can arise. For instance, a partnership between two Rebels might be fraught with power struggles and a lack of stability, as both partners may resist compromise and authority.

Friendships also reflect the influence of archetypes. A friendship between an Explorer and a Sage, for example, might thrive on shared adventures and intellectual discussions, with each friend bringing out the best in the other. However, tensions can arise if one archetype dominates the relationship. For instance, if one friend consistently takes on the Ruler role, making decisions and setting the agenda, the other might feel stifled or undervalued. Recognizing these dynamics can help you navigate friendships more effectively, fostering mutual respect and understanding.

In family dynamics, archetypes often define roles and expectations. A parent with a dominant Ruler archetype might naturally assume a position of authority, guiding the family with a firm but fair hand. Meanwhile, a child with a strong Explorer archetype might seek independence and new experiences, sometimes clashing with the parent's need for order and control. Understanding these patterns can help family members appreciate each other's strengths and work together more harmoniously.

Communication is key to navigating archetypal dynamics in relationships. Openly discussing each person's dominant archetypes and how they manifest can lead to greater understanding and empathy. For example, if you recognize that your partner or friend identifies strongly with the Sage archetype, you might approach them for advice and value their perspective on complex issues. Similarly, if you understand that a family member is driven by the Rebel archetype, you might give them the space they need to express their individuality while finding common ground on important matters.

Ultimately, understanding the role of archetypes in relationships allows for more intentional and compassionate interactions. By recognizing and respecting each other's archetypal influences, you can build deeper, more meaningful connections with those around you.

Archetypes in Culture and Society
Archetypes are not only personal symbols but also cultural forces that shape the narratives of our societies. They are embedded in our myths, literature, films, and even in political and social movements. This section explores how archetypes influence culture and society, providing insights into the broader implications of these symbolic patterns.

In the realm of literature and film, archetypes serve as the foundation for storytelling. The Hero's journey, for example, is a narrative structure that resonates across cultures and time periods. This archetypal story, popularized by mythologist Joseph Campbell, involves a protagonist who embarks on a quest, faces challenges, and undergoes a transformative experience. Characters like Luke Skywalker in *Star Wars* and Harry Potter in *The Harry Potter Series* exemplify this archetype, reflecting universal themes of courage, sacrifice, and personal growth.

The Rebel archetype is also prevalent in cultural narratives, particularly in stories of social and political change. Characters like Katniss Everdeen in *The Hunger Games* and V in *V for Vendetta* embody the Rebel's defiance of oppressive systems and their fight for justice. These characters resonate with audiences because they reflect the human desire for freedom and the courage to challenge the status quo.

In politics, leaders often embody the Ruler archetype, projecting authority, control, and a vision for the future. Figures like Winston Churchill and Franklin D. Roosevelt are celebrated for their leadership during times of crisis, embodying the Ruler's ability to guide and protect their people. However, the shadow side of the Ruler archetype can also manifest in tyranny and authoritarianism, as seen in historical figures like Napoleon Bonaparte or Joseph Stalin.

Social movements often draw on the energy of the Rebel archetype, challenging existing power structures and advocating for change. The Civil Rights Movement in the United States, led by figures like Martin Luther King Jr., exemplifies the positive aspects of the Rebel archetype, as it sought to dismantle systemic racism and promote equality. However, movements driven by the Rebel archetype can also become destructive if not guided by a clear vision and ethical principles.

Understanding the role of archetypes in culture and society allows us to recognize the underlying patterns that influence collective behavior. It also empowers us to engage with these narratives more consciously, choosing to align ourselves with stories and movements that reflect our values and ideals. Whether in literature, film, politics, or social activism, archetypes continue to shape the way we understand the world and our place within it.

Using Archetypes for Personal Growth
Archetypes are powerful tools for personal growth and self-improvement. By consciously working with your archetypes, you can harness their energy to overcome challenges, achieve your goals, and become the best version of yourself. This section provides practical strategies for using archetypes to facilitate personal development and transformation.

To begin, set clear intentions for what you want to achieve through your work with archetypes. Whether your goal is to build confidence, develop stronger relationships, or pursue a creative passion, identify the archetypes that can support you on your journey. For example, if you seek to cultivate more confidence, the Hero archetype can help you tap into your inner strength and courage. The Lover archetype, on the other hand, can support you in building deeper connections and embracing your emotional needs.

Once you have identified the relevant archetypes, create a plan of action that incorporates rituals, practices, and exercises aligned with those archetypes. For instance, if you are working with the Creator archetype, you might set aside time each day for creative activities such as writing, painting, or music. These practices allow you to express your creativity and connect with the deeper aspects of your personality.

If the Sage archetype is central to your personal growth, you might engage in activities that foster wisdom and insight, such as reading philosophical texts, meditating, or participating in discussions on complex topics. These practices can help you develop a deeper understanding of yourself and the world around you, leading to greater self-awareness and enlightenment.

It is also important to be mindful of the shadow side of each archetype and the potential challenges that may arise. For example, the Sage archetype can lead to detachment or isolation if not balanced with compassion and connection. To avoid these pitfalls, make an effort to stay connected with others and practice empathy in your interactions.

Personal growth is a continuous process, and as you evolve, your archetypes may shift or take on new forms. Stay open to this evolution and continue to explore the depths of your inner world. The more you engage with your archetypes, the more you will uncover the rich tapestry of your personality and the limitless potential within you.

Through understanding, balancing, and integrating your archetypes, you can lead a more intentional, authentic, and fulfilling life. These timeless symbols offer a pathway to deeper self-awareness, richer relationships, and a more meaningful connection to the world around you. By embracing your archetypes, you step into your true power and begin the journey toward wholeness.

Archetypal Assessment: The Orisha-Archetype Indicator (OAI)

Introduction
The Orisha-Archetype Indicator (OAI) is a psychometric tool designed to help individuals identify the dominant archetypes that influence their behavior, motivations, and perspectives. Drawing upon the archetypal framework proposed by Carl Jung and integrating the rich symbolism of the Orisha from African traditional religions, the OAI offers a unique approach to self-discovery and personal growth.

Purpose and Background
The purpose of the OAI is to provide insight into the archetypal patterns that shape an individual's psyche. By identifying these patterns, users can gain a deeper understanding of their intrinsic motivations, strengths, and challenges. The OAI builds upon the work of Carl Jung, who proposed that archetypes are universal, primordial images and themes present in the collective unconscious. This assessment also draws on the rich tradition of African spirituality, particularly the Orisha, which are powerful spiritual beings that embody specific archetypal qualities.

As noted by Awo Fa'lokun Fatunmbi in his exploration of Ifa and the Orisha, "the Orisha represent archetypal forces that guide the lives of individuals, shaping their destinies in ways that are both personal and universal" (Fatunmbi, *Hermeneutics - African Traditional Religions: Ifa*, 1993, 45). By combining these two traditions, the OAI offers a holistic approach to understanding the self.

Structure of the OAI
The OAI consists of a series of statements that respondents rate on a scale of 1 to 5, where 1 indicates strong disagreement and 5 indicates strong agreement. These statements are designed to assess the prominence of

various archetypes in the respondent's life. The OAI includes twelve archetypes, corresponding to both Jungian archetypes and their Orisha counterparts:

1. The Innocent – Yewa
2. The Orphan/Everyman – Oya
3. The Hero – Shango
4. The Caregiver – Yemaya
5. The Explorer – Ochosi
6. The Rebel – Ogun
7. The Lover – Oshun
8. The Creator – Orishaoko
9. The Jester – Elegua
10. The Sage – Orunmila
11. The Magician – Osanyin
12. The Ruler – Obatala
13. The Martyr – Obba Nani

Scoring and Interpretation

After completing the assessment, respondents will receive scores for each archetype, indicating the degree to which each archetypal pattern is active in their lives. High scores suggest that the corresponding archetype is a dominant influence, while lower scores indicate lesser influence.

Conclusion

The OAI is a powerful tool for self-reflection and personal development. By exploring the interplay between Jungian archetypes and the Orisha, users can gain a richer, more nuanced understanding of their inner world.

Instructions:

This assessment consists of 52 statements. Rate each statement on a scale from 1 to 5, where 1 indicates strong disagreement, and 5 indicates strong

ARCHETYPAL ASSESSMENT

agreement. Answer as honestly as possible to gain the most accurate understanding of your archetypal influences.

Scale:
1 - Strongly Disagree
2 - Disagree
3 - Neutral
4 - Agree
5 - Strongly Agree

---

1. The Innocent / Yewa
1. I strive to maintain peace and harmony in all areas of my life.
2. Purity and innocence are qualities I deeply value in myself and others.
3. I believe in the inherent goodness of people.
4. I often act as a mediator, bringing calm to tense situations.

2. The Orphan / Oya
5. I sometimes feel like I am on my own, even when surrounded by others.
6. Emotional sensitivity is a defining aspect of my personality.
7. I have a deep need to belong and be accepted by those around me.
8. I am often attuned to the emotional needs of others and offer comfort.

3. The Hero / Shango
9. I am willing to confront challenges head-on, no matter how difficult they may be.
10. Strength and determination are essential traits I strive to embody.
11. I take pride in protecting those who are vulnerable or in need.
12. I am not afraid to fight for what I believe is right.

4. The Caregiver / Yemaya
13. I feel a strong sense of duty to take care of others.
14. Nurturing and providing for those in need is a natural part of who I am.
15. I often put others' needs before my own, even at my own expense.
16. I am seen by others as a source of emotional support and stability.

5. The Explorer / Ochosi
17. I am constantly seeking new experiences and knowledge.
18. Freedom and independence are very important to me.
19. I enjoy exploring new ideas, places, and perspectives.
20. I am comfortable with change and often embrace it.

6. The Rebel / Ogun
21. I believe that endings are necessary for new beginnings to occur.
22. I am not afraid to make drastic changes if it means progress.
23. I often challenge the status quo and disrupt the norm.
24. Transformation is a theme that recurs in my life.

7. The Lover / Oshun
25. Passion and intensity characterize my relationships.
26. I seek deep, meaningful connections with others.
27. I value beauty, love, and pleasure in life.
28. I am often driven by my emotions and desires.

8. The Creator / Orishaoko
29. Creativity is a core part of who I am.
30. I am driven to bring new ideas, projects, and creations into the world.
31. I find fulfillment in expressing myself through art, writing, or other creative outlets.
32. I often feel inspired to innovate and improve existing ideas or systems.

ARCHETYPAL ASSESSMENT

9. The Jester / Elegua
33. I enjoy making others laugh and finding humor in life.
34. I often challenge conventions and norms through wit and humor.
35. I value spontaneity and living in the moment.
36. I believe in the importance of not taking life too seriously.

10. The Sage / Orunmila
37. I am committed to lifelong learning and wisdom.
38. I often seek to understand the broader context or bigger picture in any situation.
39. Knowledge and truth are the primary goals I pursue.
40. I value insight and understanding above material success.

11. The Magician / Osanyin
41. I believe in the power of transformation and change.
42. I am drawn to spiritual practices and esoteric knowledge.
43. I often seek to understand the deeper mysteries of life.
44. I have a strong intuition that guides me in my decisions.

12. The Ruler / Obatala
45. I feel a strong sense of responsibility to lead and guide others.
46. Order and structure are important to me in both personal and professional settings.
47. I strive to create stability and security in my environment.
48. I am comfortable making decisions and taking charge in group situations.

13. The Martyr / Obba Nani
49. I often sacrifice my own needs to help others.
50. I believe in enduring hardships for a greater cause.
51. I am willing to bear burdens for the benefit of those I care about.
52. Self-sacrifice is a virtue that I hold in high regard.

Scoring Instructions:
1. Sum the scores for each set of 4 statements to calculate your total score for each archetype.
2. The archetype with the highest score is your dominant archetype, indicating it has the strongest influence on your personality and behavior.
3. Lower scores represent archetypes that are less dominant but may still influence you in specific contexts.

Interpreting Your Results:

The Innocent / Yewa: A focus on peace, harmony, and maintaining purity.

The Orphan / Oya: Emotional sensitivity, a desire for belonging, and nurturing connections.

The Hero / Shango: Strength, determination, and protection of the vulnerable.

The Caregiver / Yemaya: Nurturing, selflessness, and emotional support.

The Explorer / Ochosi: Exploration, freedom, and embracing change.

The Rebel / Ogun: Embracing transformation and challenging the status quo.

The Lover / Oshun: Passion, deep connections, and the pursuit of beauty and love.

The Creator / Orishaoko: Innovation, creativity, and bringing new ideas to life.

The Jester / Elegua: Humor, spontaneity, and challenging norms.

The Sage / Orunmila: Pursuit of knowledge, wisdom, and understanding.

The Magician / Osanyin: Transformation, spiritual knowledge, and intuition.

The Ruler / Obatala: Leadership, responsibility, and creating order.

The Martyr / Obba Nani: Self-sacrifice, endurance of hardships, and dedication to a cause.

Chapter 17
Conclusion

Recap of Key Points

Throughout this book, we have explored the profound significance of archetypes in shaping human behavior, personality, and life experiences. Archetypes, as universal symbols and patterns, provide a framework for understanding the complexities of the human psyche and the shared experiences that unite us all. By examining the primary Jungian archetypes—The Innocent, The Orphan/Everyman, The Hero, The Caregiver, The Explorer, The Rebel, The Lover, The Creator, The Jester, The Sage, The Magician, The Ruler, and The Martyr—we have gained insights into the various facets of our personalities and how these archetypal energies influence our thoughts, emotions, and actions.

The journey through these archetypes has highlighted the strengths and weaknesses inherent in each one. For instance, The Hero teaches us about the importance of courage and determination but also warns against the dangers of arrogance and overextension. The Caregiver embodies compassion and selflessness, yet must guard against tendencies toward martyrdom and self-neglect. The Explorer encourages us to seek new experiences and embrace change, but also reminds us of the risks of aimlessness and restlessness. Each archetype offers valuable lessons and serves as a guide for navigating the complexities of life.

Understanding our dominant archetypes allows us to gain greater self-awareness and recognize the patterns that shape our behavior. This awareness is the first step toward personal growth and transformation. By embracing the positive aspects of our archetypes and addressing their shadow sides, we can achieve a more balanced and harmonious existence. The exercises and rituals presented in each chapter provide practical tools for aligning with these archetypal energies, helping us to cultivate their strengths and mitigate their challenges.

Moreover, archetypes play a significant role in our relationships, influencing how we interact with others and the dynamics that unfold in various social contexts. Recognizing the archetypal patterns in ourselves and others allows us to navigate relationships with greater empathy and understanding. Whether in romantic partnerships, friendships, family dynamics, or professional settings, the insights gained from archetypal analysis can enhance our connections and promote healthier, more fulfilling interactions.

Archetypes also extend beyond the personal realm, influencing culture and society at large. They are the building blocks of the stories we tell, the myths we create, and the social movements that shape our world. From literature and film to politics and activism, archetypes serve as a lens through which we interpret the world around us and our place within it. By understanding these symbolic patterns, we can engage more consciously with the cultural narratives that define our society and contribute to positive change.

Final Thoughts
The journey of self-discovery through the lens of archetypes is both enlightening and transformative. As we delve into the depths of our psyche, we uncover the rich tapestry of our inner world, revealing the diverse energies that drive our thoughts, emotions, and actions. This exploration is not merely an intellectual exercise; it is a deeply personal and spiritual journey that leads to greater self-awareness, empowerment, and fulfillment.

Each archetype represents a different aspect of the human experience, offering unique insights and lessons. By embracing these archetypal energies, we connect with the universal themes that unite us all, transcending cultural and individual differences. The process of identifying, understanding, and integrating our archetypes is a lifelong endeavor, one that requires continuous reflection, adaptation, and growth.

CONCLUSION

As we move forward on this path, it is important to remember that no single archetype defines us. We are complex beings, shaped by a multitude of influences and experiences. Our dominant archetypes may shift over time, reflecting the changing circumstances of our lives and our evolving sense of self. By remaining open to this evolution, we allow ourselves to grow and transform, continually becoming more aligned with our true essence.

The wisdom of the archetypes guides us toward a more authentic and meaningful existence. It encourages us to embrace our strengths, confront our fears, and cultivate the qualities that will lead us to our highest potential. Whether we are seeking to overcome challenges, build stronger relationships, or contribute to the greater good, the archetypes provide a roadmap for personal and collective growth.

As we conclude this exploration of archetypes, it is important to acknowledge that the journey does not end here. The insights and tools gained from this book are just the beginning. The real work lies in applying these lessons to our everyday lives, using them as a foundation for continuous self-improvement and spiritual development. By integrating the wisdom of the archetypes into our daily practices, we can create a life that is not only fulfilling but also deeply connected to the broader currents of human experience.

Further Reading and Resources

For those who wish to delve deeper into the study of archetypes and their applications, there is a wealth of literature and resources available. The following recommendations provide a starting point for further exploration, offering a range of perspectives on archetypal theory, psychology, and spirituality.

1. ***Archetypes and the Collective Unconscious* by Carl G. Jung**: This seminal work by Carl Jung is foundational in the field of Jungian

psychology, introducing and expanding on the concept of archetypes and the collective unconscious. Jung explores how these universal patterns influence the human psyche, shaping behaviors, dreams, and cultural narratives. The text delves deeply into the nature of archetypes, illustrating their role in the collective unconscious and their profound impact on individual and collective experiences. It is an essential read for anyone seeking a comprehensive understanding of Jungian psychology and the enduring power of archetypal symbolism.

2. *The Hero with a Thousand Faces* by **Joseph Campbell**: Joseph Campbell's seminal work on the Hero's Journey provides a comprehensive analysis of the Hero archetype and its manifestation in myths and stories across cultures. This book is essential reading for anyone interested in the role of archetypes in storytelling and personal development.

3. **"The Pearson-Marr Archetype Indicator (PMAI)" by Carol S. Pearson and Hugh Marr**: The PMAI is a popular self-assessment tool designed to help individuals identify their dominant archetypes. This book provides a detailed explanation of the PMAI and how it can be used for personal growth and self-discovery.

4. *Women Who Run with the Wolves: Myths and Stories of the Wild Woman Archetype* by **Clarissa Pinkola Estés**: This powerful book explores the Wild Woman archetype through a collection of myths and stories, offering insights into the instinctual and intuitive aspects of the feminine psyche.

5. *King, Warrior, Magician, Lover: Rediscovering the Archetypes of the Mature Masculine* by **Robert Moore and Douglas Gillette**: This book examines the four archetypes of mature

masculinity, providing a framework for understanding the development of the male psyche and its archetypal influences.

6. ***The Power of Myth* by Joseph Campbell and Bill Moyers**: Based on a series of interviews between Joseph Campbell and Bill Moyers, this book explores the enduring power of myths and their relevance to modern life. It offers valuable insights into the role of archetypes in shaping cultural narratives and personal identity.

7. **Courses and Workshops**: For those who prefer a more interactive approach to learning, many institutions and organizations offer courses and workshops on archetypal psychology, mythology, and related topics. Online platforms such as Coursera, edX, and The Jungian Institute provide access to a wide range of courses that can deepen your understanding of archetypes and their applications.

By engaging with these resources, you can continue your exploration of archetypes and their profound impact on the human experience. Whether through reading, self-assessment, or interactive learning, the journey of self-discovery and growth through archetypal analysis is a rewarding and transformative path.

As I bring this exploration to a close, I find myself deeply humbled by the vastness and richness of the journey we've undertaken together. Throughout these pages, I've aimed to bridge the wisdom of Carl Jung's archetypes with the profound spiritual heritage of the Orisha, revealing how these ancient energies continue to shape our lives, our culture, and our personal growth.

This book is not just a culmination of research and insight; it is also a reflection of my own personal journey—a path filled with discovery, challenge, and transformation. My hope is that you, too, have found your own path illuminated by the stories, teachings, and exercises presented here. I encourage you to continue engaging with these archetypes and the Orisha in your own life, using them as guides to navigate the complexities of the human experience.

Remember, this work is never truly finished. The process of self-discovery, much like the cycles of nature, is ongoing. As you move forward, may you carry with you the knowledge that within each of us lies the potential for growth, healing, and profound connection to something greater than ourselves. Thank you for allowing me to accompany you on this journey, and I wish you every success as you continue to explore and integrate the wisdom of the archetypes and the Orisha into your life.

Glossary

1. **Anima/Animus**: Jungian terms referring to the feminine inner personality (anima) present in the male psyche and the masculine inner personality (animus) present in the female psyche. Balancing these aspects is key to psychological health.

2. **Archetypes**: Universal, symbolic figures or motifs found in myths, stories, and dreams, representing different aspects of the human experience. In Jungian psychology, archetypes are seen as innate, universal prototypes that shape human behavior.

3. **Candomblé**: An Afro-Brazilian religious tradition that combines elements of Yoruba, Bantu, and Fon spirituality with Roman Catholicism. Candomblé involves the worship of orishas, spirits that represent natural forces and ancestors.

4. **Carl Jung**: A Swiss psychiatrist and psychoanalyst who founded analytical psychology. Jung is known for his concepts of the collective unconscious, archetypes, and individuation.

5. **Collective Unconscious**: A part of the unconscious mind shared among beings of the same species. According to Jung, it contains memories and impulses of which the individual is unaware, common to all humankind.

6. **Eborí Eledá**: A concept related to the orisha tradition, representing the spiritual head or guardian consciousness of an individual. It is another name for the "Rogacion de Cabeza," a ritual that involves spiritual cleansing and blessing of the head to align with one's spiritual path and guardian orisha.

7. **Elegua**: The orisha of crossroads, doors, and communication in Yoruba religion. Elegua is considered the guardian of the roads and paths and is often the first orisha invoked in ceremonies.

8. **Individuation**: The process by which an individual becomes distinct and integrated, achieving personal psychological wholeness. This is a central concept in Jungian psychology.

9. **Lukumi**: A term used to describe the Yoruba-derived religious practices and traditions in Cuba, also known as Santería.

10. **Obatala**: The orisha of wisdom, purity, and creation in Yoruba religion. Obatala is considered the father of all orishas and is associated with peace and calmness.

11. **Obba Nani**: An orisha associated with marriage, fidelity, and domesticity in Yoruba religion. Obba Nani is often depicted as a symbol of devotion and sacrifice.

12. **Ochosi**: The orisha of hunting, justice, and the wilderness in Yoruba religion. Ochosi is known as a protector of those who seek truth and justice.

13. **Ogun**: The orisha of iron, war, and labor in Yoruba religion. Ogun is associated with strength, resilience, and the power to overcome obstacles.

14. **Orisha**: Deities or spirits in the Yoruba religion, each embodying specific natural forces and human characteristics. They serve as intermediaries between the human world and the divine.

15. **Orishaoko**: The orisha of agriculture and farming in Yoruba religion. Orishaoko is associated with fertility, the earth, and the sustenance of life.

16. **Orunmila**: The orisha of wisdom, knowledge, and divination in Yoruba religion. Orunmila is regarded as the master of Ifa, the divination system that provides guidance and insight.

17. **Osanyin**: The orisha of herbal medicine and healing in Yoruba religion. Osanyin is associated with the knowledge of plants and their medicinal properties.

18. **Oshun**: The orisha of love, fertility, and rivers in Yoruba religion. She is associated with beauty, harmony, and sensuality, often embodying the Lover archetype.

19. **Oya**: The orisha of winds, storms, and transformation in Yoruba religion. She represents the Orphan/Everyman archetype, associated with resilience and the ability to navigate life's challenges.

20. **Rogacion de Cabeza**: A ritual within the orisha tradition involving the cleansing and blessing of an individual's head to promote alignment with their spiritual path and connection to their guardian orisha.

21. **Santería**: A syncretic religion of Yoruba origin, practiced primarily in Cuba, which combines elements of Catholicism with the worship of orishas.

22. **Shango**: The orisha of thunder, lightning, and fire in Yoruba religion. He is often depicted with a double-headed axe and symbolizes strength, virility, and power.

23. **Shadow**: The unconscious part of the personality that contains repressed weaknesses, desires, and instincts. Confronting and integrating the shadow is crucial for personal growth.

24. **The Caregiver**: An archetype characterized by compassion, generosity, and a desire to help others, often representing the nurturing aspect of the human experience.

25. **The Creator**: An archetype that embodies creativity, imagination, and the desire to bring something new into existence. This archetype values originality and self-expression.

26. **The Explorer**: An archetype driven by a desire for discovery, adventure, and new experiences. It represents the quest for self-discovery and pushing boundaries.

27. **The Hero**: An archetype representing courage, strength, and determination. The Hero embarks on a journey, faces trials, and ultimately achieves a transformative victory.

28. **The Innocent**: An archetype characterized by optimism, simplicity, and trust, representing a childlike purity and a sense of wonder in the world.

29. **The Jester**: An archetype associated with humor, playfulness, and the ability to bring joy to others. The Jester often uses humor to cope with life's challenges.

30. **The Lover**: An archetype focused on building relationships, passion, and connection. The Lover values intimacy, beauty, and the fulfillment of emotional needs.

31. **The Magician**: An archetype that represents transformation, insight, and the ability to see beyond the ordinary. The Magician often seeks to harness unseen forces to create change.

32. **The Orphan/Everyman**: An archetype representing the universal human experience of belonging, realism, empathy, and connection.

33. **The Rebel**: An archetype associated with defiance, independence, and challenging the status quo. The Rebel seeks to bring about change and reform.

34. **The Ruler**: An archetype focused on control, order, and leadership. The Ruler strives to maintain stability and authority within a structure or society.

35. **The Sage**: An archetype representing wisdom, knowledge, and the pursuit of truth. The Sage seeks to understand the world through learning and reflection.

36. **The Martyr**: An archetype that embodies sacrifice, selflessness, and the willingness to endure suffering for a greater cause. The Martyr often represents the ultimate commitment to one's beliefs.

37. **Yewa**: A Yoruba orisha associated with purity, chastity, and the cemetery. She embodies the Innocent archetype in the book's framework.

References

Abimbola, Wande. *Ifa: An Exposition of Ifa Literary Corpus*. Ibadan: Oxford University Press, 1976.

---. *Ifa Will Mend Our Broken World*. Aim Books, 1997.

Barnes, Sandra T. *Africa's Ogun: Old World and New*. 2nd ed. Bloomington: Indiana University Press, 1997.

Bascom, William. *Ifa Divination: Communication between Gods and Men in West Africa*. Bloomington: Indiana University Press, 1991.

---. "Shango in the History of Yorubaland." In *African Arts*, vol. 3, no. 4 (Summer 1970), pp. 8-13+71.

---. *Sixteen Cowries: Yoruba Divination from Africa to the New World*. Bloomington: Indiana University Press, 1980.

Bolen, Jean Shinoda. *Goddesses in Everywoman: Thirteen Powerful Archetypes in Women's Lives*. Harper & Row, 1984.

Campbell, Joseph. *The Hero with a Thousand Faces*. Princeton: Princeton University Press, 1949.

Drewal, Henry John. *Yoruba: Nine Centuries of African Art and Thought*. The Center for African Art in Association with Harry N. Abrams, Inc., 1989.

Drewal, Henry John, and Margaret Thompson Drewal. *Gelede: Art and Female Power among the Yoruba*. Bloomington: Indiana University Press, 1983.

Facina, Adriana. "Jung at the Crossroads or Reading Jung from Exu." *Junguiana* 41, no. 3 (2023): 25-38.

Fatunmbi, Awo Fa'lokun. *Hermeneutics - African Traditional Religions: Ifa.* Accessed July 14, 2024. https://atla.libguides.com/c.php?g=1138564&p=8384915.

Gleason, Judith. *A Recitation of Ifa, Oracle of the Yoruba.* New York: Grossman Publishers, 1973.

---. *Oya: In Praise of an African Goddess.* San Francisco: HarperSanFrancisco, 1992.

Hamilton, Edith. *Mythology: Timeless Tales of Gods and Heroes.* New York: Little, Brown and Company, 1942.

Idowu, E. Bolaji. *Olodumare: God in Yoruba Belief.* Longman, 1962.

Jung, Carl G. *Psychology and Alchemy.* Princeton: Princeton University Press, 1980.

---. *The Archetypes and the Collective Unconscious.* Princeton: Princeton University Press, 1959.

Lawal, Babatunde. *The Gelede Spectacle: Art, Gender, and Social Harmony in an African Culture.* Seattle: University of Washington Press, 1996.

Love, Velma E. *Divining the Self: A Study in Yoruba Myth and Human Consciousness.* Penn State University Press, 2012.

Mason, John. *Four New World Yoruba Rituals.* Brooklyn: Yoruba Theological Archministry, 1992.

Miller, Ivor. *Voice of the Leopard: African Secret Societies and Cuba.* Jackson: University Press of Mississippi, 2009.

Murphy, Joseph M. *Santería: African Spirits in America.* Boston: Beacon Press, 1993.

---. *Working the Spirit: Ceremonies of the African Diaspora.* Beacon Press, 1994.

Olmos, Margarite Fernández, and Lizabeth Paravisini-Gebert. *Creole Religions of the Caribbean: An Introduction from Vodou and Santería to Obeah and Espiritismo.* New York: New York University Press, 2003.

Original Botanica. "Shango and Oya: The Power of Love and Unity." Accessed July 27, 2024. https://www.originalbotanica.com/blog/shango-and-oya-the-power-of-love-and-unity.

Pearson, Carol S., and Hugh Marr. *The Pearson-Marr Archetype Indicator.* Gainesville: Center for Applications of Psychological Type, 2003.

Thompson, Robert Farris. *Flash of the Spirit: African and Afro-American Art and Philosophy.* New York: Vintage Books, 1983.

Yacub, Moyeen. *Yoruba Mythology and Archetypal Psychology: Orisha as Transformational Symbols.* Greenwood Press, 1998.

Index

- **Anima/Animus** - Pages 12, 15, 47, 102, 145
- **Archetypes** - Pages 5, 21, 29, 45, 61, 97, 113, 150, 171, 191
- **Candomblé** - Pages 85, 149, 212
- **Carl Jung** - Pages 1, 7, 13, 17, 100, 145, 213
- **Collective Unconscious** - Pages 18, 22, 49, 103, 160
- **Eborí Eledá** - Pages 218, 220
- **Elegua** - Pages 98, 127, 150
- **Individuation** - Pages 23, 29, 55, 60, 145, 250
- **Lukumi** - Pages 85, 149
- **Obatala** - Pages 88, 103, 134, 176
- **Obba Nani** - Pages 116, 120, 136
- **Ochosi** - Pages 101, 115, 119, 136
- **Ogun** - Pages 100, 115, 152
- **Orisha** - Pages 14, 32, 65, 85, 149, 213
- **Orishaoko** - Pages 92, 104, 133
- **Orunmila** - Pages 95, 109, 140
- **Osanyin** - Pages 92, 112, 141
- **Oshun** - Pages 102, 120, 143
- **Oya** - Pages 97, 113, 129, 153, 190
- **Rogacion de Cabeza** - Pages 220, 221
- **Santería** - Pages 85, 149, 211
- **Shango** - Pages 100, 115, 152, 180
- **Shadow** - Pages 30, 48, 66, 85, 117, 191
- **The Caregiver** - Pages 71, 95, 117, 151
- **The Creator** - Pages 131, 153, 177
- **The Explorer** - Pages 87, 101, 136
- **The Hero** - Pages 55, 79, 102
- **The Innocent** - Pages 25, 49, 77
- **The Jester** - Pages 149, 155
- **The Lover** - Pages 115, 139, 166
- **The Magician** - Pages 191, 205
- **The Orphan/Everyman** - Pages 41, 75, 98, 135
- **The Rebel** - Pages 101, 128, 157
- **The Ruler** - Pages 213, 225, 230
- **The Sage** - Pages 171, 189, 202
- **The Martyr** - Pages 229, 246, 250
- **Yewa** - Pages 29, 45, 49, 102, 12

About the Author

Jonathan "Afolabi" Baker has been an adherent of the Lukumí faith since 2007 and is a crowned priest of Yemayá. He holds a master of science degree in psychology (2015) along with training in vocational evaluation, life coaching, and cognitive behavioral therapy (2017-2019), culminating in a doctoral degree in 2022. He is internationally-certified in his field and provides vocational evaluation services to individuals with disabilities throughout the state of Florida. He is a South Florida native and a coffee aficionado. When not working, he spends time with his wife, children, and dogs.

Made in the USA
Columbia, SC
17 August 2024

8fb3085b-2b13-4025-b931-8a61f9b547e0R01